TO HAVE AND TO HOLD

D1630745

02
03/08

30130503947742

TO HAVE
AND
TO HOLD

Marriage,
the first baby
and preparing couples
for parenthood

CHRISTOPHER F CLULOW
in collaboration with
Evelyn Cleavely, Patricia Coussell
and Barbara Dearnley

ABERDEEN UNIVERSITY PRESS

First published 1982
Reprinted 1989
Aberdeen University Press
A member of the Pergamon Group

© The Tavistock Institute of Medical Psychology, London, 1982

British Library Cataloguing in Publication Data
Clulow, Christopher F.
To have and to hold: marriage, the first baby
and preparing couples for parenthood.
1. Parenthood   2. Marriage
I. Title
306.8'74   HQ755.83

ISBN 0 08 028470 1
ISBN 0 08 028471 x (flexi)

PRINTED IN GREAT BRITAIN
THE UNIVERSITY PRESS
ABERDEEN

Foreword

by Dr JOHN BOWLBY

As a result of the combined efforts of research workers in many countries over the past half-century, there is no longer difficulty in specifying the conditions which promote the development of stable, co-operative and self-reliant children and adults. Children develop best in stable families in which both mother and father are able and willing to give them plenty of time, attention and encouragement and in which the parents pull together in harmony. This conclusion is hardly new; but it is now supported by such an impressive weight of evidence that it is no longer easy for critics to contest.

But it is one thing to specify these conditions and another for parents to provide them. Most parents, I believe, sincerely wish to provide favourable conditions for their children's development but all too often, we know, they get into difficulties. How then can we best help them? Although over the years a great deal of valuable work has been done, no one believes it to be sufficient. In what ways therefore can it be improved?

When a couple have their first baby the honeymoon is over and the work begins. Not only that, but both parents discover afresh that where two is company three can make for friction. Strong feelings are aroused and old conflicts relighted. A new equilibrium has to be found.

In this book Christopher Clulow describes an attempt to find means for helping parents through this transition. In collaboration with the health visitors of the district, social workers from the Institute of Marital Studies set up evening discussion groups to which couples expecting their first child were invited. To what extent, they wondered, could current knowledge of how people cope with major changes in their lives be used to help the couples cope with the great change shortly coming to them. Could useful help be given in a limited number of evenings during the last months of pregnancy and the early months of the newly-created threesome, limits selected to take account of the constant pressures of a health visitor's life?

The experiences of the workers are recounted both vividly and candidly. Much was learned—not only about what new parents can and cannot digest during the transition period but also, in a series of workshop meetings, about

the prodigiously varied and difficult tasks expected of health visitors. Perhaps
the most valuable outcome of the project for the participating couples was that
it put them in touch with neighbours experiencing a similar transition and with
the professional workers available to help them. Yet once more the vital
importance emerges of continuity in the individuals who provide care and also
of the merits of small units—two basic principles constantly at odds with
administrative convenience.

In traditional communities when a baby is born a mother receives a great
deal of help from her own mother and other women of that generation.
Fortunately, that pattern still persists in many parts of our society and, where it
does, is to be cherished. All too often, however, young couples live isolated
from kith and kin and hardly knowing their neighbours. For them new
arrangements are necessary.

One of the most promising lines of future advance, I suspect, is the
development of parents' self-help groups, supported by a health visitor who is
personally known to members and available to give skilled assistance when
required. In demonstrating the potentialities of self-help among families the
pre-school playgroup movement has blazed a brilliant trail. And at a
theoretical level social scientists now recognise more clearly that the ready
availability of a familiar person, trusted to respond helpfully when required, is
one of the most valuable of social commodities. Nothing gives us more
confidence to utilise our own capabilities to the full than the knowledge that
when we are in a fix we are not alone.

Nevertheless, invaluable though the development of self-help groups may
prove to be, there will always be families where more is required. Some of them
can seek help and use it; others both want it and reject it. This poses a great
problem for the professional workers engaged. Readers will be grateful not only
for the light the author throws on such problems but also for his description of
a way by which they can be approached. Understanding a problem is a first step
to solving it.

Contents

Acknowledgements

Many people have participated in and advised upon the work described in this book. Of these I particularly want to acknowledge the extensive contribution made by my three colleagues, Evelyn Cleavely, Patricia Coussell and Barbara Dearnley, who, with me, formed the team which planned, undertook and evaluated the project.

As a group we are indebted to those health visitors and managers of the Ealing, Hammersmith and Hounslow Area Health Authority who were hosts to the project and fellow participants in the discussion groups and workshop meetings. They have contributed to the book in many different ways. Through Miss Marian Strehlow, the Council for the Education and Training of Health Visitors supported the project in its early stages and commented upon the manuscript in its draft form. To her, and the Council, I am grateful.

My thanks go to those couples who, through the group and questionnaire, shared some of their impressions of parenthood with us. In particular, I want to express my appreciation to Mr and Mrs Grant, and Mr and Mrs Good, who know themselves by other names, and who gave me permission to write about an unsettled and sometimes distressing period in their lives.

The project would not have been possible without the generous financial support of the Leverhulme Trust Fund. The Institute of Marital Studies, which receives its major grant from the Home Office, also contributed towards the cost.

My colleagues in the Institute of Marital Studies carried additional work while the project was running and commented on the manuscript. I thank them, and especially Janet Mattinson who helped me in putting pen to paper. I am also most grateful to Maureen Rooney, my dependable secretary, who serviced the project from first proposal to final manuscript.

Of those outside the Institute of Marital Studies I would like to acknowledge the help given by Dr Ian Sinclair who, while he was a member of staff, prepared the ground for the project and subsequently acted as our consultant. Members of the Institute of Marital Studies Advisory Panel of the Tavistock Institute of Human Relations provided helpful comment on the text. I particularly want to acknowledge the help given by the late Dame Eileen Younghusband in the early stages of the project, by Professor Gordon Dunstan whose interest and advocacy have been a constant source of encouragement, and by Mr Nicholas Tyndall who supplied the phrase which most eluded me in describing a concept central to the thesis, and which I have taken for the title of this book. Mrs Isabel Menzies Lyth and Mrs Elmer Sinclair offered helpful comment on the manuscript, as did Mrs Margaret Stoneman on the research chapter. The project initiated a series of meetings between the Institute and the Marriage Research Centre at the Central Middlesex hospital; we enjoyed and profited by the discussions we had with Dr Jack Dominian and his colleagues.

Mrs Margaret Walker and her staff at the Tavistock Joint Library were, as always, most helpful. Ortho Pharmaceutical Ltd very kindly lent me their film *Sexuality and Communication* for the duration of the project.

I am grateful to Faber and Faber Ltd, and Harcourt Brace Jovanovich Inc. for permission to quote some lines from 'The Journey of the Magi' in *Collected Poems 1909-1962* by T S Eliot–copyright 1936 Harcourt Brace Jovanovich Inc, copyright 1963, 1964 T S Eliot; to William Heinemann Ltd and David Higham Associates Ltd in connection with the line I have used from *Books Do Furnish a Room* by Anthony Powell; to Routledge and Kegan Paul and the University of Chicago Press for the use of a passage from Arnold van Gennep's *The Rites of Passage*, translated by Monika B Vizedom and Gabrielle L Caffee in 1960; and to Martin Robertson and Company Ltd for permission to reproduce a quotation from *Becoming a Mother* by Ann Oakley.

Finally, I want to thank Pamela, my wife, for bearing with me during the writing of this book and reminding me, when I was in danger of forgetting, that home is not an extension of the office. With her, and through our two daughters, I have learned what it means to be a parent. For all the ups and downs, it is an experience I would not be without.

Prologue

This book is about the transformation in marriage which follows the birth of a first child and the implications of that transformation for those who seek to prepare couples for parenthood.

In the excited anticipation of life with a baby, it is common for parents to overlook the passing of hitherto important aspects of life as a couple. Yet marriage is changed by parenthood. Change involves loss as well as gain.

This mixture of loss and gain featured in the replies of fifty-seven couples to a questionnaire* which asked for a personal assessment of the effect of parenthood upon marriage. The enquiry was undertaken in order to assemble a range of first-hand impressions which might be useful to couples who were themselves about to become parents. A selection of these impressions forms an appropriate prologue to this book, which is concerned with the transmission of experience in the service of others.

The comments which follow have been selected because they represent and express the wide range of views contained in the replies. They are presented as a collection of personal snapshots contributed by parents who, for their own reasons, were interested in sharing their impressions. These snapshots have been assembled into a montage representing some of the diversity of experience which comprises the reality of early family life. In order to allow the material to speak for itself there is no commentary or linking sequence, and no attempt has been made to draw conclusions.

* See Appendix I for further details.

xiii

Pregnancy . . .

Kicks . . .

'From the minute I knew I was pregnant I was tremendously happy, I felt
very elated right through pregnancy. I felt physically well and enjoyed it.
Also, the timing was right and we were both excited.'

'The high spots were when I got bigger and there was something to show!
When baby kicked and we could feel her. When my husband took care of
me and did things for me, like washing my hair.'

'I think my husband would say that I never looked so radiant. Apart from
feeling and looking so well I was able to keep working, and I think this helped
us both. We didn't really have any low spots as I kept so well, and the greatest
times were when our baby started to let me see him as active—he used me as a
football net and my husband used to think this was great.'

and kicks . . .

'. . . having to go to work until five weeks before birth; feeling very big and
with swollen ankles; giving up sex in later months; attending the hospital
and doctors so frequently; the worry that something may go wrong; will we
be able to manage on one salary?'

'. . . morning sickness; frequent backache; difficulty in sleeping
comfortably; tendency to tearfulness.'

'I found it was very thrilling at first when I realised I was pregnant and had
got used to the idea. But as I started getting bigger in size I felt very
unattractive, and at the end I would say I really disliked pregnancy
intensely, especially when I went 'over' the original date given me for the
birth.'

and no kicks . . .

'During the first seven months I kept active with hobbies and tried not to think too much about the baby. I'm pessimistic, and would often say I'll believe it when I see it. The last two months were worrying because complications arose.'

'Because I tended not to believe in my pregnancy (only so that there would be less explaining if anything were to go wrong) there were no initial feelings of elation or depression.'

'I had an easy pregnancy and life was relatively normal as I worked until two weeks before the birth. We moved house when I was six months pregnant so there was much activity and planning; the fact that I was pregnant didn't really register with either of us.'

feeling and talking . . .

'We found we had trouble talking about what we would do if our baby was born not normal. We always ended up saying not to talk about it or even think about it.'

'There was very little hope of talking rationally about my state of mind and it didn't help to ramble on, upsetting others.'

'I felt very tired often—some books say this is depression. I didn't see it as specifically feeling depressed—didn't think I was.'

'. . . a feeling of loneliness after I had to give up working.'

'Last two or three weeks of pregnancy were very bad. I felt very depressed and rather useless. My husband didn't seem to understand and was rather impatient with me.'

sex . . .

'My husband enjoyed me physically throughout my pregnancy which helped tremendously.'

'Sex ceased at about four months because my husband could not get sexually aroused and my sexual drive dwindled.'

'No intercourse took place during pregnancy so as not to disturb anything, but there was plenty of lovemaking.'

'I felt as if I were being mauled the whole time and got to the point I could not bear to be touched.'

'The absence of need for any precautions during pregnancy made it more enjoyable, although towards the end it was rather uncomfortable.'

sex and the baby . . .

'In pregnancy we were advised to have no intercourse for the first twenty weeks in case of miscarriage. This had a lasting effect on my husband who was terribly afraid he might hurt the baby. I think we both felt that if this pregnancy were not successful we may not succeed in future to have a child.'

'. . . after (the first two or three months of pregnancy) my husband suggested that we stopped intercourse as he did not want to chance anything. This consideration and concern both for me and the unborn baby pleased me, as I was slightly worried that something might go wrong.'

'After the "morning sickness" I felt quite sexual, but as the pregnancy developed I began to feel there were three of us; two voluntary, one without choice.'

'We found it difficult to express ourselves within the relationship and particularly sexually. The pregnancy made this more difficult simply because of the idea that it was wrong to make love when someone was in there.'

Birth

'The birth itself was the most exciting thing I've ever experienced.'

'The birth was a fantastic experience that we both shared.'

'. . . my husband stayed with me through my labour and held my hands. When I gave birth (he) saw her and heard her cry.'

'We both felt bereft at the birth—Julie was born by Caesarian section, under epidural, after twenty-one hours in labour, most of which we managed with no drugs. John was terrific the whole time but he didn't see his daughter born. We were both very deflated after the months of build up to the birth.'

'(I remember) the pain I felt in labour, and the stitches.'

'I had more courage at the birth than we both could have imagined.'

'Being at the birth totally changed me and my outlook on life for the better.'

'I found the moment of birth an enormously emotional experience, as did my husband, and was 'high' for several days and came down with a bump a few days later. My husband was very worried about me then and later I had to go to psychiatric hospital which was a greater shock for him than for me. I was back in 'cloud cuckoo land'. . . . '

And After

the baby . . .

'A loud sneeze from the other bedroom one morning confirmed that she, another person, was there.'

'Babies do not recognise Sunday as being different from any other day!'

'I was totally unprepared for the pain when the milk came and the emotional upheaval I went through when I got the baby home . . . until my health visitor arrived two weeks after I got home I saw no-one, it was a terrifying experience and I can't be the only one.'

'. . . if my husband had not been able to take ten to twelve days holiday immediately after I came back from the hospital things might not have gone as well as they did.'

the new parents . . .

'I have found we don't argue like we used to. I think I used to argue to liven things up. Now things are too lively all the time. We haven't had a big row since he was born.'

'We never used to argue until the baby was born, but she took so much out of us the first six to eight months due to illness and not needing sleep, that we just felt we needed to take out the pent up feelings on someone.'

'There seems to be less time for our relationship since the birth. I feel my husband needs more reassurance about the baby's feelings for him than I do. I suppose I have more confidence in her feelings for me because I'm with her all day.'

'I have realised how easily I can be pushed to the limit and how fine the line is between controlled and uncontrolled behaviour. At this point my husband has taken control until I could carry on with the child.'

'I can honestly say that for the first six months the baby put a tremendous strain on both my husband and myself as individuals, and on our marriage as well.'

'I used to be very independent, but now I do need my husband's support in both a material and emotional sense. In fact, we just had a bit of a row about this as I cannot stand anymore the detached attitude he sometimes takes. I had been at home all day and when he got in I told him I had been weeding the garden, etc., and he only said: "Did you really?" This made me cross. My husband has always been like that, but now I feel I cannot stand it as well as I used to.'

'I feel the baby has brought us closer together. When we were both working we were like two individuals. Now we have something to share apart from our home.'

work . . .

'Our roles are defined as never before. He is the breadwinner and I am the homemaker. Intellectually we remain as before but emotionally we have matured. His role remains as it always was, the breadwinner but with greater responsibility. Mine is new and I have to come to terms with it, not working, and not earning money.'

'Although money is freely handed between us it's not the same as having a regular income that you've earned.'

'. . . at eight months I returned to part-time work, which was a mistake, as I felt I had to look after the baby, work and run the house. This created a little possibly unjustified resentment against my husband, who has since tried to help more with the baby and with shopping, etc. I intend to give up work when I have completed my notice.'

'I work both from choice and necessity. Although I do not feel guilty about having made this decision I find that other people, particularly mothers,

tend to assume that if I can cope with a baby, full-time job, house, etc.,
. . . I must either do things badly or be exceptional. I resent this. . . . '

'(I) lost my job and my freedom, but gained love for a baby that I never
thought I would have, as I was never child-minded.'

'Being a mum and homemaker seems to have no status in our society.
You've suddenly become a parasite, a brainless individual who is of no
benefit to society. This is the biggest single handicap I have to live with. My
professional friends treat me as though I can no longer think or express an
opinion, that my place is "down the clinic talking babies"! And the worst
of it is that I felt like that before wanting to have a baby. What has
happened to us that we should believe that motherhood means automatic
removal from society? Those friends without children no longer invite you
because you have become a nuisance, you have a baby that cries, interrupts
an ordered existence. But they lose out, not us. It's just hard to understand
that you are not as acceptable as before.'

who does what for the baby . . .

'When the baby is crying, it is generally the one with the most patience at
the time who deals with the problem.'

'My husband has more patience than me with the baby. But he had more
contact with children. Children never interested me before my own child
was born.'

'We all get up at 8.30 am and while my wife changes the baby I get
dressed, then come down for breakfast (coffee and toast), then rush out. I
get home by about five, by which time dinner's been made for the baby
and me. The baby goes to bed at seven.'

'I, being the mother, fully accept that I should do everything for the baby
and get great pleasure from it.'

'I do it all unless I'm out, and then my husband takes over, if it's not for
too long a period.'

'I have discovered that it takes a lot of effort to be a fully participating
father and that I have at times to make a conscious decision to help.'

'I often feel I ought to do more, but never strongly enough to do so for any length of time. . . . I'm afraid I do as little as my conscience will let me.'

'We feel that the baby has in fact benefited from an excellent childminder. . . . I needed to go back to work early (i.e. at two months) before I became too settled in home/baby routine.'

feeling and talking at this stage . . .

'I found it *easier* to talk about things which I normally find difficult.'

'I think when you are really depressed you don't want to talk to anyone about anything.'

'I was rather ashamed of getting angry with my baby so I did not tell anyone.'

'I remember feeling very "alone" all the time. There was never anyone to "turn to". We were never a family to say or show our love for each other.'

'. . . showing my feelings about the whole situation (is difficult), and talking about coming to terms with problems which existed in our relationship before and after the birth. So much was said in my wife's childhood—her parents argued all the time and finally divorced. My parents kept emotions secret and feelings weren't discussed. So neither of us, for different reasons, seems able to confront the problems.'

'Unfortunately my husband is not a talker, and least of all he talks about his own feelings. No chance of his doing this questionnaire! He often gives the impression that he does not care, as he does not talk. This hurts me sometimes.'

'. . . there were times when I needed to talk things out with someone else, especially with friends who had already had babies.'

sex after birth . . .

'. . . our sexual relationship was affected by the sheer exhaustion caused by the work and broken nights a baby brings.'

'We did not have sex for about ten weeks and it was a while after that before I enjoyed it. The main reasons for not having intercourse were continual tiredness and soreness. My husband would stay up and give the baby his late night feed and I went to bed early and got up to give the early morning feed, so we weren't often awake in bed at the same time.'

'Six weeks after the birth my husband and I had intercourse. I was quite frightened that the stitches would not take. I knew my husband was also frightened about hurting me. Now those fears have ceased.'

'In early parenthood you just have to get past the first time and the feeling that it is going to be painful, especially if you have had quite a few stitches.'

'After the birth we had no trouble and resumed our normal sexual relationship.'

'Having the baby has demolished a good healthy sex life, and it is now at a very dangerous edge of not being repairable.'

'. . . I found that my sexual appetite increased during the early months of parenthood.'

'. . . my interest waned a little as I didn't need to prove I was still desirable.'

sex and babies . . .

'I found that I was terrified of becoming pregnant again.'

'. . . at weekends, with the baby pottering about, I feel we cannot indulge when we feel like it because she seems to be watching, which puts me off.'

'After the birth we did not resume relations for two months, and for a few months after I found it difficult to view my husband as I had before. This new image was firstly that of a father, rather than a sexual partner.'

'Our problem was my inability to explain what I felt or meant and my husband's persistent requests for explanations, because of his inability to understand the mental and physical changes taking place during and after pregnancy. For my husband, because I had had a baby, I should then have been quite normal apart from "post-natal depression" which he was all ready to deal with. When I wasn't co-operative about sexual intercourse he thought that I didn't care.'

a new look at the past . . .

'The first time I saw Mark talking to his teddy in his cot brought back so many memories of my "pretend" people as a child."

'About all it makes me remember is what it was like to be physically small so that rooms and objects seemed large. Makes me feel too big for the rooms now, sometimes.'

'I remember how lonely I often was and would like to protect my daughter from that—I was an only child with no father. I remember how much I envied my friends who had proper families and how much I wished I had the general "hurly-burly" of family life in my own home and very much want her to be happy in her home, and for it to be a haven for her.'

'I missed my father as a child—away at the war; still do; nothing can replace this. Perhaps I try to make up to her what I missed.'

'I wasn't close to my mother, so now I am really going to try and develop a good relationship with my daughter.'

'No-one seemed to remember anything about me when I was a baby.'

a new look at the present . . .

'I gained an understanding, a new awareness towards everybody, not only my husband, with regard to people's feelings. They're all somebody's sons or daughters and I would hate anybody to hurt my son with some carelessly chosen words.'

'A sense of excitement and curiosity in the most mundane of things.'

'. . . less negative and pessimistic about life in general.'

'I'm still surprised how much she interests me as I've never been too interested in other people's children—and I'm still not.'

'For me, I have new-found security and a strength I didn't realise I had. I feel much more direct as a person. There is a strong bond in our relationship which was not there before. We are now a family—and that's a new and positive feeling.'

a new look at partners . . .

'I have now seen a completely different side to my husband's character—a gentleness which I would have found hard to believe beforehand.'

'I didn't realise my husband was as selfish as he was until the baby was born. Although we both wanted her he seems to let me do everything. "A woman enjoys it," he says, but doesn't realise I need a break now and again, too. When he wants to go out he just goes, when I want to go out on my own for a while it's a catastrophe.'

'I discovered another side to his personality and I find that his concern and pride for the baby reflects on me. . . . He seems genuinely happy to be a father and it gives an extra dimension to the relationship.'

'My husband is very patient and very loving towards her—he has surprised me. She is all things to him now. He is planning for her future and he wants her to have a good life. He doesn't say much in words but it is so obvious. He is very emotional at times about her. It would be very nice to have a son for his sake—we would not be so 'over-protective' and emotional about two children, I feel.'

a new look at parents . . .

'As the child grows up you hear yourself saying the things that your parents said to you and that you vowed and declared you would never say to a child of yours and you realise why they said them . . . but I believe that we shall always be their children.'

'Both sets of parents have become more concerned with the baby than with us. Our reaction to their possessive nature has been to become more possessive of the baby.'

'I think my relationship with my mother has improved since the baby's birth . . . (she) has been happier than I've ever seen her.'

'I'm closer to them now as I understand how they'd feel if anything happened to me, because I know what having a child means now.'

'We see that our parents consider us to be more on their level and talk to us more freely.'

'It has made parents' relations on my wife's side improve from Bloody Diabolical to VERY GOOD.'

swings and roundabouts . . .

'We have obviously had to stop going out for tête-à-tête meals and stay in a lot more; but that's no hardship as we can't afford it now! We have become a lot closer since our daughter was born, and we think the fact that we were both there for the induction, labour and birth, cemented us right from the start.'

'We have given up the freedom to choose where we go and when we go, as consideration must be given to meal times, and whether a baby, pram, etc, is acceptable. Each outing is a major expedition and not just a question of up and away. This can be a strain on the relationship, as before you have only each other to consider.'

'There were days we could not sit down and have a drink together. All the routine changed to suit the baby. But we both did not mind as this is only for a year at the most. We feel our married life is more secure than ever because being a very happy family we discovered we had more love and respect for each other.'

'We have given up what we would term "spontaneous living", that is, doing what we wanted, when we wanted.'

'I feel we have only really become a "family" since my daughter was born, as opposed to a couple of individuals who are married.'

Introduction

The birth of a first baby marks an important revolution in the family life cycle. It is a significant moment of generational change. There must follow a reorganisation of relationships, both inside and outside the family, to allow for development of the new roles and different satisfactions which children bring. The light in which new parents appear to themselves and to others will alter in consequence, and may be transformed in ways which are quite unexpected. Together, the social significance and personal meaning of parenthood critically affect the ability of parents to behave as they might wish or plan in relation to each other and to their offspring.

The social and personal implications of change can be mediated through the relationship of marriage. The word 'marriage' refers here, and subsequently, to the relationship between co-habiting parents, whether legally solemnised or not. This partnership affects how the transition to parenthood is managed, and is, in turn, affected by that transition. It has potential to influence whether the legacy of the past is handed on unchanged to future generations, or whether there is sufficient room for a creative response to the challenge of a new family life.

This book is concerned with the reasons for adopting a maritally-oriented approach to parenthood preparation and the implications of an attempt, made between 1977 and 1979, to implement a service for couples expecting their first child. The work was undertaken by the Institute of Marital Studies,* in collaboration with a group of London health visitors. It began for three principal reasons.

In the first place, clinical experience accumulated within the Institute suggested that many couples who sought help there did so as a result of difficulties which could be traced back to the time when they first became parents. Sometimes they came for help soon after the birth of their first child. Sometimes years had elapsed before the situation reached a point where professional help was required. Usually their problems were complex and not easy to explain. Often the partners had planned and worked together for a family, and were sufficiently well-off not to be unduly affected by material hardship once their baby was born. Yet the experience of parenthood had, in

---

* The Institute of Marital Studies is an organisation which offers a therapeutic service to couples experiencing difficulties in their marriage and which, through training and research, is committed to the development of effective practice in other branches of the helping professions.

the words of one mother, acted like a 'volcanic eruption', leaving the partners divided, angry, hurt and uncomprehending about a change in their lives which, as it had been imagined in prospect, should have served to bring them together. Their experiences posed the question of why something potentially so good had turned out to be so bad. Just as important, they aroused interest in discovering how widespread the problem was, and in learning what might be done to bridge the gap between expectation and experience so that the impact of children upon marriage might be less distressing.

Sifting through relevant research studies, it became apparent that starting a family was a stressful experience for many more people than those who found their way to the doors of the helping professions. While many of these studies concentrated their attention upon the relationship between a mother and her baby, those which took account of marriage indicated not only that a significant change took place in that relationship as a result of parenthood, but also that marriage exercised an important influence upon the capacity of parents to adapt to their new roles and altered circumstances. These findings provided a second reason for considering what action might be taken to facilitate the transformation in family relationships which follows the birth of a first child.

Finally, there was a political impetus to consider ways in which the *Cycle of Deprivation* might be broken. This phrase was used by the Secretary of State for Social Services in 1972 to describe the transmission of disadvantage from one generation to the next. Since then, the need for preparation for parenthood, as one means of intervening during a key period of change in the family life-cycle, has been referred to in a number of government reports.

The chapters which follow trace the process by which four members of the Institute of Marital Studies (hereafter referred to as the project team) decided to adopt a marital approach to parenthood preparation, and describe their experience of translating this approach into practice. The book is divided into two parts.

Part I, entitled *Marriage and Parenthood*, considers why this particular period of family change warranted the setting up of a prophylactic service. Chapter One presents an interpretative account of the experiences of two couples who came to the Institute for help shortly after the birth of their first child. Their case histories serve to highlight both the need for, and the complexity of preparing for events which may turn out very differently from what is imagined in prospect. In this chapter, marriage is seen primarily as a psychological relationship, with a capacity to contain the tensions and conflicts which events can precipitate in the individuals concerned. For the couples described, that capacity was temporarily overtaxed and they sought the containment of outside help.

Chapter Two takes a wider view of marriage and parenthood as it appears from the research literature. While some differences exist between researchers, parenthood is portrayed in a very different light from the soft-focus world of the commercial advertisement. Taken together, clinical experience and research evidence make a case for a marital approach to parenthood preparation. In doing so, it may seem as if some of the positive and rewarding aspects of family life are given too little prominence. The purpose is, however, to draw attention to what might be described as the unacceptable face of parenthood, and so to establish that there is a need to be met.

Part II, entitled *An Approach to Parenthood Preparation*, describes an action research project which set out to test one method of helping first-time parents to manage the transition from two to three. This method incorporated a direct and indirect approach to couples. Chapter Three explores the questions and issues which shaped the work. Chapter Four details a group approach to preparing couples for parenthood, as it was implemented in four London family health centres. Chapter Five considers some of the opportunities for, and constraints upon, health visitors in their individual work with families, as they appeared from workshop discussions. In the light of the main findings, Chapter Six reviews assumptions upon which the project was based, and reconsiders the meaning of preparation and prevention in connection with promoting the emotional health of families.

In brief, the project found that first-time parents can be helped by creating and supporting a social milieu in which preoccupations occasioned by the birth of a first child might be shared and taken seriously. During pregnancy, informal contact between prospective parents, and between couples and their health visitors, was valued by both sides. Ante-natal contact served to establish relationships which could subsequently be drawn upon if, and when, the need arose. By developing a social safety net for couples, and by offering a service which spanned pregnancy and the early months of parenthood, the discussion groups added an extra dimension to existing classes.

However, the degree to which it was possible to anticipate the emotional impact of a baby upon the parents as individuals, and upon their marital partnerships, was very limited in these groups. The evidence indicated that parenthood had to be experienced before its implications could be fully appreciated. Troubling aspects of that experience were more likely to be disclosed in retrospect than at the time, and in private rather than to an assembled group.

Consequently, the health visitor's role during the early months of parenthood became the focus of the project's attention. From the workshop discussions it was apparent that parents do talk to health visitors about the psychological and social stresses of parenthood, although not always in a direct manner. The willingness and capacity of health visitors to pick up indirect messages, and to respond appropriately to them, was related to the type of support and training they receive for doing so. The workshops provided a forum in which it was possible for health visitors to be helped to pick up indirect communications, and to articulate conflicts in their role which, when managed well, could result in an effective and integrated service to families. As such, the workshops provide a model for a safety net for health visitors, enabling them to involve themselves with families without undue fear of losing their professional identity in the process.

It is with some of the questions which consider how far people can afford to talk, and to listen, to each other, that this book is principally concerned. Those looking for ready solutions to the problems of preparing couples for parenthood, and caring for the family at this turning point in its history, are likely to be disappointed. The endeavour established, for couples and health visitors alike, a forum in which their preoccupations might be articulated, and in which they were encouraged to find their own solutions through drawing upon their experience, and that of others.

Throughout the book there runs a common thread in the concept of *containment*, which links marriage, birth and the endeavour to prepare couples for parenthood. The underlying assumption is that certain kinds of relationships are better suited than others to contain the experiences of everyday life. Containment is a less than perfect word to describe the process involved because of its restrictive connotations. It is, however, used to describe a process which encourages expression and life in relationships while at the same time providing a sufficient measure of security to ensure that experience is not over-powering. Marriage, as a close and continuous relationship, affords particular opportunities for generating life within a secure social framework. The inter-course between two people which results in the birth of a baby symbolises the creation and management of new life which the word containment is intended to convey, a process which is well described by a phrase in the marriage ceremony: *to have and to hold.*

PART ONE

Marriage and Parenthood

All this was a long time ago, I remember,
And I would do it again, but set down
This set down
This: were we led all this way for
Birth or Death?

T S Eliot

CHAPTER ONE

Two Couples

It is not what happens to people that is significant, but what they think happens to them.

Anthony Powell

The starting point for the venture described in this book was the knowledge that, for some couples, the birth of a first baby resulted in marital difficulties serious enough to warrant their seeking professional help. This chapter will examine the experiences of two such couples, for whom parenthood, quite contrary to their expectations, precipitated tensions which they were unable to manage alone. The accounts are interpretative, and therefore some mention of the assumptions which inform them is necessary.

AN INTERPRETATIVE FRAMEWORK

Writing as a novelist, Anthony Powell distinguishes between inner and outer realities when he infers that the same event can be experienced differently by different people. These differences can be explained by examining the personal frames of reference which are applied by individuals to make sense of what they see and hear. At the Institute of Marital Studies, the psychodynamic model which informs therapeutic practice holds that an individual's perception of his world derives from a highly personal interpretation of past experience. His selective account of history will unwittingly emphasise certain features and obscure others. In this way, what a person thinks happens to him in the present, and therefore how he behaves in relation to events, is substantially affected by past influences of which he may or may not be aware.

Marris (1974) and Parkes (1971) have studied these personal windows on life with particular reference to the process of change. Marris writes about a 'structure of meaning' to describe the framework assembled by a person over the years to make sense of his life experience. Parkes uses the term 'assumptive worlds' to describe a similar idea which, in his words, 'includes our interpretation of the past and expectations of the future'. Both concepts substantially define who we are as people, and how we are likely to behave in different situations. They provide us with bearings in uncharted territory, and therefore are not lightly to be discarded.

Yet most people are capable of up-dating and modifying their personal windows on life. In the course of development, perceptions are shaped and modified by our interaction with the social, cultural and material world of which we are a part. Our experience of important events like marriage, birth, divorce or bereavement, has to be accommodated within the particular frames of reference we have developed over time. Sometimes change requires relatively little modification of our view of ourselves and others. Sometimes, our experience of an event and the assumptions we rely upon to make sense of life are so discrepant as to be profoundly unsettling. Marris calls these discrepancies crises of 'discontinuity', adding that some cohesion between our expectations and experience of events is crucial if change is to be managed creatively, for 'without continuity we cannot interpret what events mean to us, nor explore new kinds of experience with confidence'. A crisis of 'discontinuity' is essentially a crisis of identity.

Events have significance not only within a current context of meaning, but also, by re-evoking previously obscured aspects of the past, through their ability to undermine the foundations upon which our perceptions are based. From Freud's (1896) account of the 'return of the repressed' in the lives of his patients to present-day psycho-analytic thinking, there runs a common thread, which acknowledges the importance in current perceptions and behaviour of past influences of which we are unaware. In summarising the development of one approach to understanding unconscious processes of this kind, Sutherland (1963) draws attention to the potential of close relationships to resurrect purposefully forgotten aspects of previous relationships with the confusing result that history can sometimes be inappropriately relived rather than remembered as belonging to a separate and distinguishable past. Taking this dimension into account, events have a capacity to challenge our assumptions about ourselves and our worlds, not simply by introducing a dissonant note in current experience, but by disturbing and re-awakening previously obscured aspects of the past which threaten the organisation of our basic structures of meaning at their very roots.

Some tension between our assumptions about life and our current experience of people and events is potentially creative; without it there is no stimulus for change and development. Tension must, however, be kept within manageable proportions if development is to be assisted and not inhibited.

The capacity of an individual to contain the tension resulting from conflicting experience is importantly affected by his social environment. Close relationships, of which marriage is arguably the most important, are likely to be especially significant. In the present, they can provide help and support in coping with the stresses of everyday life. Marriage in particular, as 'the most direct heir of the intense primary relationships of childhood' (Pincus, 1960), allows for a recreation and reworking of the past within an intimate, present-day, adult partnership. There is, in that respect, an opportunity for both partners to check their bearings in order that personal frames of reference may be re-aligned to cope more effectively than before with the demands of change.

The ability of relationships to bring hidden conflicts to life, and to manage the tension and anxiety aroused in the process, constitutes their capacity to act as a *container*. In this context, the word 'container' refers to those relationships which exhibit a permissiveness and tolerance which facilitate past and present conflicts coming to life, and a benign 'holding' structure which can withstand the resulting tension. Marriage is a potentially effective 'container' in these terms.

In the two accounts which follow, the birth of a first baby regenerated feelings of such intensity in the parents that their capacity to act as they wished in relation to each other and their children was temporarily over-taxed. For a time, outside help was needed to help them manage the conflict. Their different experiences combine to support the view that the birth of a baby is not of itself responsible for the stressful period through which some couples subsequently live; it is the meaning of that event in the light of their present circumstances and personal histories which is important in understanding why the same event can be experienced by parents in so many different ways.

The couples who appear in this chapter have read and assisted in the documentation which follows; they have consented to the material being made public in this way. Needless to say, details which might threaten their anonymity have been disguised or omitted.

MR AND MRS GRANT

Birth

Lisa was born ten months after Mr and Mrs Grant were married.

Mrs Grant had wanted a baby for a long time. Her husband had agreed, with some reluctance, that once they were married they would stop using contraceptives. She welcomed her pregnancy and, because she was fit, she worked until four weeks before the baby was born. During pregnancy she had some nagging doubts about whether she really wanted to be a mother, but she did not allow herself to worry unduly. Yet she was concerned that from the fourth month of pregnancy she lost interest in sex.

Together Mr and Mrs Grant attended the one ante-natal class to which husbands were invited. They planned a natural childbirth, without analgesics, and were agreed that Mr Grant should be present at birth. In the event, Mrs Grant had a protracted labour and a forceps delivery which meant that neither parent witnessed Lisa's birth. When she awoke from the anaesthetic, Mrs Grant did not know she had given birth. She was very disappointed not to have been conscious when her daughter was born and she became depressed in hospital, thinking that perhaps she ought not to have had a baby after all. Conversely, with his daughter's arrival Mr Grant was won over to the notion of parenthood. He saw Lisa five minutes after she was born and felt it was one of those rare moments in life when 'everything is put right'. He was overjoyed with the baby and felt that a longing inside himself had been satisfied.

Mrs Grant left hospital with her baby to return to their two-roomed flat. From then on, life became increasingly difficult. She felt unprepared for the hard work of looking after a baby and isolated in her surroundings. Their flat was one of a block designed for single people or working couples, and there were no other mothers with young children living there. Although Mr Grant helped to look after Lisa when he came home from work, Mrs Grant found she was becoming more and more irritable with him and with her daughter. While she wanted a baby, she was not sure she wanted to be a mother. When Lisa was nine months old, she returned to work.

At first, the break from motherhood was a relief, and Mrs Grant managed to recover something of her former self. Her firm ran a nursery, and because this was nearer to Mr Grant's office than her own, he took Lisa to and from the nursery each day. He became increasingly involved with her and Mrs Grant began to feel that she had little time to enjoy her daughter in the way that her husband obviously did; instead she felt left with making sure bedtimes and meal-times were regularly observed. Moreover, she became bored with her work, but she did not think she could face full-time motherhood again.

The strain showed in their marriage. Mrs Grant became irritable and withdrew from her husband. Their sexual relationship remained infrequent and half-hearted, as it had been since the fourth month of her pregnancy. When Lisa was twenty-one months old Mr Grant wrote to the Institute of Marital Studies asking for help.

The referral

Mr Grant's written application drew attention to the triangular nature of the problem:

> There are at least three difficulties that coincide to bring about a lot of stress on us this winter. First, for complicated reasons of conveyancing, our flat will not be saleable until April at least, so we are stuck in cramped quarters.
>
> Second, my wife is unhappy with her job but cannot leave it because we need the nursery place subsidized by her employer.
>
> Third, now that Lisa is coming to be a little aware of herself as a person, I get to worry that she will suffer from not having sufficient affection from her mother, my wife being a person who finds it hard to be affectionate at times.

If we had just two of these three problems, we might be all right. But if we do not get some guidance we might take a hard fall under the stress of all three. On paper it looks easy to plan a way forward. But on the ground our emotions are harder to control and we are neither of us very confident, or forceful, personalities. For these reasons, guidance is needed.

In her written outline, Mrs Grant amplified the emotional aspects of their problem, which might be expressed in terms of there being too little space in their marriage for three people:

The immediate problem is that we live in a two-roomed flat and we are getting on each other's nerves. My husband stays even-tempered mostly, but I scream at him and Lisa as soon as they do something that annoys me. We should at some point move to a bigger flat, but I don't think that alone will mean harmony. I must have the place clean, and if I don't I can't stand it. When we are both at home with Lisa she must feel some tension and always runs to her father to be picked up or comforted. This upsets me, although when I'm alone with Lisa we get on perfectly alright. My husband does, in fact, see Lisa more than I do. This is out of necessity because he takes and collects her from the nursery. I am stricter with Lisa regarding bed-time, table-manners and how often she should be picked up.

I am not happy about my relationship with Lisa, nor that with my husband. It sometimes seems to me that I am angry with Lisa to annoy my husband. For some reason I want to see how far he will tolerate my screaming and shouting and occasionally hitting him. I don't think I want to stay at home with Lisa, but I don't really like my job either—why don't I change my job? One reason has been given by my husband (the immediate practical one) and the more important reason is that I don't know what else to do and I feel I could not do anything else.

Personal histories

Mr Grant, at that time a self-preoccupied man of thirty-one years, summarised their problem as his wife's inability to respond affectionately towards Lisa. While he enjoyed looking after his daughter, whom he described as a 'shining light', he thought the mother's role was crucially important, and could 'make or break a child's future'.

Asked about his own experience as a child, Mr Grant painted a picture of an isolated boy whose parents, for different reasons, were never available enough for him. Although he had an elder and younger brother he seldom made reference to them and centred his attention firmly upon his parents, for whom he had great admiration and, it seemed, a still unsatisfied longing.

During the early years of his life the family lived abroad and relied heavily upon their own resources. At the age of twelve, after returning to England, Mr Grant felt he lost both his parents. His mother was less available to him through ill health, while his father became more distant from the family than before, spending an increasing amount of time away from home. Pressed about his mother, who was still alive, Mr Grant became tearful and said he doubted if anyone could really understand the pain he had experienced in the past. It had resulted in a turbulent adolescence. Mr Grant described himself as a 'drop-out child of the sixties'; at university he had consulted a psychiatrist because he thought he was going to pieces. It was his wife, he thought, who had managed to put him back together again.

Mrs Grant was three years younger than her husband, but displayed a composure and realism about life which made her seem older than him. Her pale complexion and long hair gave her an almost madonna-like appearance.

She defined the problem as her difficulty in knowing whether or not she wanted to be a mother. She had wanted a baby very much, but being a mother had left her feeling unhappy and disillusioned. Work had provided a temporary respite from these feelings but no solution to their problem. In some respects it had served to aggravate her sense of isolation in the family, and she looked upon the relationship between her husband and Lisa with a mixture of envy and disapproval. In particular, she disapproved of her husband's indulgence, although she knew that he thought she was too strict and cool in her approach to their daughter. Mrs Grant thought that their different approach to Lisa was the main area of conflict in the marriage. Whereas she could manage Lisa on her own, when all three were together she would become very angry, and would take out her feelings on either her husband or her daughter.

Sometimes Mrs Grant wondered if their problems were simply the result of living in cramped accommodation. She likened their flat to a transit station, designed for one or two people, but certainly not a family home. However, she thought there was more to it than that. She was worried that she felt no sexual drive and feared that her lack of interest might drive her husband into the arms of someone else. She had thought things would improve once the baby was born, or when she stopped breastfeeding, but in neither case did this happen.

In her own family, Mrs Grant was the elder of two girls; her sister was two years younger than herself. For the first thirteen years of her life she was brought up in Germany because her father worked there. At first she described him as a strict man who had wanted little to do with children. Later, she talked about how she had thought when she was young that they got on well together, but her mother had told her he was never interested in her. Her parents separated when she was nine years old and both girls stayed with their mother.

In her early years, Mrs Grant was brought up by a German nanny, while her mother went out to work. As a result she learned to speak both English and German fluently. When Lisa was born Mrs Grant found that she spoke to her daughter almost exclusively in German, as if that were her mother tongue. To her husband and other people, she generally spoke English. She thought her two 'mothers' might have relevance to her dilemma between staying at home with Lisa or returning to work. She talked about wanting her daughter to think she was 'worthwhile', in the same way that she admired her own mother. She feared that if she stayed at home, she would become uninteresting to others, and particularly to her daughter. This low estimation of herself can be attributed in part to a feeling of not having been sufficiently interesting to her parents to keep them at home and together. Her unsatisfied longing was once picked up by Mr Grant when he asked why someone who had seen relatively little of her mother as a young child should be so attached to her in later life.

Mrs Grant said that orderliness was important to her and that this obsession had dated from her sister's birth. Her mother's view was that she had reacted to her sister's arrival by becoming a perfectionist, and Mrs Grant thought that was probably true. She said that her mother treated each of them exactly alike. Mrs Grant made a direct connection between her behaviour towards Lisa and that towards her sister when she added that she used to scream at her sister in German when she lost her temper. Furthermore, she connected her husband with her sister when she said that it was important to her that he should not be treated as special, or in any way different from herself. Referring to Mr Grant's secret hurt, his wife once expostulated: 'He thinks because of that thing he is somebody special—and he is *not* special. I don't think I am special so I don't think he should be special.'

The marriage

Mr Grant first met his wife through a friend. He was nineteen at the time and discovered that their two families were acquainted. Some time later, each learned that the other had planned to study abroad for a year in the same country; Mrs Grant telephoned him to suggest they travelled out together. While Mr Grant had been attracted to her when they first met and thought she had 'an almost mystical charm', he panicked when she telephoned him and turned her down. There followed a long chain of distant communications by letter and telephone before they met again. They were abroad at the time and Mrs Grant came to stay in his flat.

Mr Grant became very attached to her and the 'Marlene Dietrich' image that she evoked for him. He thought they communicated on the same level and he felt very alive with her. In his view she put him together after his turbulent late adolescence. Mrs Grant agreed that their relationship had met a need in each of them, as neither was overtly affectionate or able to express feelings very well. She thought he was 'very queer and strange' at the time, but 'quite liked that'.

When they returned to England Mr Grant wanted to continue the relationship, but Mrs Grant broke it off. They met a year later when he was working in London and he lodged with her in her mother and stepfather's home. 'He moved in for convenience, nothing more,' said Mrs Grant, reducing their relationship to its lowest common denominator as she often tended to do. He did, however, share her bedroom.

At first, Mr Grant was enamoured not only of Mrs Grant, but also of her family and what he experienced as the stimulus of family life in her home. Later he became disenchanted by the exclusiveness of Mrs Grant's relationship with her mother and the ordinariness of her parents' relationship when they fell out with each other. He decided to move out and Mrs Grant left with him. They bought a flat and Mrs Grant furnished it.

After some months of living together, Mrs Grant became concerned that she was making all the running in their relationship and Mr Grant was not participating. They were 'drifting', and she wanted a token of commitment from him. She also wanted to start a family and have two children, like the family she had left. When Mr Grant could be persuaded to talk about it, he said he wanted three children, as in his own family. Mrs Grant pressed for either commitment or separation.

Seven months after they had moved into their flat, they were married. Mr Grant said he felt dissociated from himself at the time, as if he were 'playing a part' in a play someone else had written. He reduced his commitment to 'paying his dues to society', but went through with the marriage. Lisa was born ten months later.

Comment

At one level, Mrs Grant's experience of becoming a mother was very similar to the experiences of many women as they appear in research findings. Her hopes of a natural childbirth were dashed by the need for special medical assistance; she became depressed in hospital (the so-called 'four-day blues'); she left hospital to return to cramped living conditions where she coped with the responsibilities of parenthood without the support of girl-friends or other mothers of her age. She felt sexually unresponsive. Her self-esteem was shaken and she returned to work in an attempt to recover her confidence and diminish her social isolation. The strain upon the marriage might be explained in terms of these factors alone.

Yet the Grants were clear that such factors were only a part of their problem and that they compounded, rather than created, difficulties which had a longer antecedent history. This was why their difficulties were particularly resistant to practical solutions. For example, what can be understood as Mr Grant's attempt to help his wife to be the sort of mother he wanted her to be, by actively involving himself as a parent with Lisa, only seemed to make matters worse. How might this be explained?

The main point of conflict in their marriage was over the handling of Lisa. Mrs Grant felt that her husband was too indulgent with the child. He felt that she was too distant and controlling. This conflict becomes understandable if Lisa is seen as the child each parent unwittingly identified within themselves. For example, Mr Grant portrayed himself as an isolated child in pursuit of a person (mother) who would understand him perfectly. In defining their problem he had stressed how important mothers were. It took little imagination to realise that when he talked about Lisa, and his concern that his wife was distant towards her, he was also talking about himself and the distant relationships he recalled in his own family. His indulgence with Lisa was therefore a way of making good what he felt he had missed in his own past. He became, as it were, the ideal mother to Lisa that he wished for himself. To allow his wife to become absorbed in Lisa was to run the risk of being left out in the cold, facing once again the familiar hurt he associated with distance in relationships.

The anomalies in his story are interesting. Why did he revere his parents yet feel they had abandoned him and were responsible for his going to pieces when he left home? If he wished to be understood, why choose such a 'distant' wife? Mr Grant expressed this particular dilemma when he remarked that there were 'thousands of girls who could have been more motherly towards me than my wife, but I chose the hard road'.

One explanation for these anomalies is that Mr Grant had, in fact, suppressed his feelings of anger about his past experiences of loss and isolation to avoid still further being cut off from those important to him, a consequence he feared if he showed his true emotional colours. His mother's breakdown and his father's drift away from the family confirmed, from his particular perspective, a suspicion that others would not be able to withstand his feelings. In these circumstances, a rosy picture of family life served to keep at bay feelings of need and dissatisfaction which were feared to be of overwhelming strength. Marriage to a 'distant' woman allowed these private dreams to go relatively unchallenged, but, at the same time, ran the risk of recreating the very conditions which were most likely to recall the frustrations of the past. The potential for development in this situation was that the past might indeed be re-evoked and reworked in the marriage, allowing Mr Grant the chance of integrating in a creative way aspects of his personality which caused him anxiety.

The birth of Lisa disturbed the illusion and polarised feelings, so that, in an effort to restore the soft focus, Mr Grant became increasingly indulgent and vulnerable. His wife became increasingly angry and remote. In this situation, Mrs Grant's behaviour can be said to reflect some of her husband's feelings, particularly his denied anger and his sense of failure in meeting self-imposed standards of parenting. In so far as Mr Grant was relating to disowned aspects of himself in his wife, the tension in the marriage was an expression of the tension within himself which had been heightened by Lisa's birth.

The traffic did not flow in one direction only. Mrs Grant presented herself as a no-nonsense realist, a woman firmly identified with her own mother who had clear ideas about order and upbringing in the home. For her, too, there were anomalies. Why was an apparently orderly and self-sufficient woman attracted to the 'strangeness' of a man who, in his own estimation, had gone to pieces? Why did the realist marry a romantic? Why did the woman who felt so identified wtih her own mother have such difficulty in asserting her maternal prerogatives once Lisa was born? As time went by it became clear that while Mr Grant feared the consequences of expressing his own irritation, and did not want to know about his own detachment (aspects of himself he criticised in his wife), Mrs Grant feared her tenderness which she located and objected to in her husband. For her, the penalty of attachment seemed to be the risk of re-experiencing earlier loss.

Lisa's arrival created for the Grants a family of three people. Threesomes had posed particular problems for Mrs Grant in the past. As a very young child she had, in effect, two mothers. Her mother employed a German nanny, and German became Mrs Grant's 'natural' mother tongue. Her dilemma between staying at home with Lisa or returning to work as her English mother had done is understandable in relation to the dual mothering she had herself received in the past.

Another threesome was created when her sister was born. Mrs Grant dated her obsessional tidiness from that event, implying that her feelings were messy enough at the time to warrant directing a considerable amount of energy towards keeping them under control. The linguistic link she made between shouting at both her sister and her daughter in German when she lost her temper suggested that the degree of her irritation after Lisa's birth owed something to her perspective upon events years earlier when her sister was born.

Again, Mrs Grant felt she had secured her mother at the expense of her father. By supporting her mother's decision to leave him, and by unquestionably accepting her mother's view of father's involvement in the family, she denied the loss which his departure represented. The seeds of her inability to interfere in Lisa's relationship with her husband may well have been sown when her mother, from Mrs Grant's perspective, came between her and her father: in her world, to have behaved like mother in that respect might have endangered Lisa's relationship with her father.

Mrs Grant's interpretation of past events was that 'two's company, three's a crowd'. It was only when she had her husband to herself that she recovered her sexual feelings, and in this sense could let go some of her controls. As a pair, Mr and Mrs Grant had in common a lack of confidence in themselves as parents. The sense of identification between Mrs Grant and her mother, and between Mr Grant and his father, was not strong. Mrs Grant, in her one criticism of her mother, complained that she had not been prepared for what it felt like to be a mother. This uneasy identification with the parent of the same sex may have added to the difficulties of assuming a familiar parental role once Lisa arrived.

Family feelings were important in attracting the Grants to each other. Lisa's birth faced them with the task of looking at family life from the other end of the telescope, so to speak, and this at a time when their marriage had scarcely been established. A shared idealism was shattered by the realities of birth and parenthood and the Grants were left with the strong feelings which follow disillusionment. One explanation for the inability of their marriage to contain these feelings is that the task of establishing a marriage had merged with that of starting a family. Without the support of the marriage, without the support of her husband *for herself*, Mrs Grant was uneasy about staying at home with her baby.

With outside assistance the Grants were able to make a good adaptation to the change in their lives and their difficulties resumed manageable proportions. An abbreviated account of their treatment and its outcome is contained in Appendix II.

MR AND MRS JACKSON

Birth

Mr and Mrs Jackson were married for nearly three years before Rose was born. Both parents wanted a baby and the pregnancy was planned. Yet her arrival precipitated what Mrs Jackson described as 'a volcanic eruption' in their lives.

Birth itself was not easy; after a protracted labour Mrs Jackson was delivered by caesarian section because the baby was lying in breech position. She remembered coming round from the anaesthetic in the early hours of the morning, but she was not told anything about her baby until well after noon. She said her husband had to insist before the baby was brought to her.

During the early weeks of her life, Rose failed to put on weight. Mrs Jackson was very worried about her, but it was only after weeks of persistently expressing concern that Rose was admitted to hospital for observation. Mrs Jackson said that, at the time, she had felt more preoccupied with thoughts of death than with the excitement of newborn life. She became depressed, in her own words, 'for much longer than I should have been'. Most of her life she had suffered from an irritable colon, and after the birth of Rose this again began to cause trouble. Mr Jackson began to remark on his wife's condition and became critical of her appearance, particularly her swollen abdomen. They began to feel they were losing each other's support.

The referral

When Rose was just over a year old, Mr Jackson was referred by his doctor to the out-patient psychiatric department of a local hospital because he had become obsessed by his wife's appearance. Mr and Mrs Jackson were seen together at the hospital. As a couple they formulated the problem in terms of Mr Jackson's obsessional personality, which resulted in critical and exacting behaviour. Since the birth of their daughter this had caused growing tension in the marriage. Mrs Jackson was hurt and angry about being constantly criticised and said she had no inclination to respond to her husband sexually. In view of the stress upon the marriage, the couple were referred by the hospital to the Institute of Marital Studies.

In outlining their problem, Mrs Jackson explained that her husband felt unable to commit his feelings to paper but that he agreed with her summary which read as follows:

Since the birth of our baby my husband has become obsessional about the appearance of my stomach. I had a caesarian section and was left with a Bowel problem which makes my stomach appear distended—part of this Bowel problem is caused by Tension, so the whole thing has got out of all proportion. I have seen two consultants who have both explained to my husband that he must learn to live with this situation, but he finds it impossible not to make some comment. This has made me ultra sensitive, and we argue constantly about this. I have completely lost interest in the sexual side of our marriage which obviously makes matters worse.

We have talked this matter out, but neither of us can reach a solution that satisfies the other one. I took tablets to lose weight, I go to 'keep fit', and take tablets to control the Bowel, but because my husband is obsessed, we are living in a state of constant upset which we both know cannot be good for us or our child.

In general terms we are a happy couple but we cannot continue in this way.

My husband admits he is obsessive but also feels I show no signs of wanting to help him—I feel he is adding insult to injury. He has been very depressed lately, and this week started a new and more demanding job which has made matters worse.

Personal histories

Mr Jackson was a lean and somewhat harassed-looking businessman working with a prestigious firm of city accountants. His dark-coloured pin-stripe suit made him look a little older than his thirty-two years. However, he had an engaging persistence and frankness of manner.

In describing their problem he dwelt upon how, for him, Rose's birth had transformed his wife from a youthful figure into a middle-aged mother. He felt the change he perceived in her was eroding his own youthfulness and vitality, and talked about his alarm at slipping into a comfortable but dead middle-aged professional existence. He worried that life was passing him by, and said that he found himself attracted to an increasing number of women. He wanted reassurance that what he called his 'ogling' was perfectly normal, and therefore, by implication, that he himself was normal. Behind his words was the suggestion that were it not for his wife he would have access to unlimited green pastures and that she was, in some sense, to blame for coming between him and the satisfaction of his unfulfilled sexual aspirations. Implied was a communication about an increasingly uncomfortable awareness of the extent of his own need, albeit recognised by him in sexual terms only.

Mr Jackson came from a working-class, lapsed Jewish background. He saw his parents as having a close, if unexpressive, partnership, although his father worked long hours and was seldom at home. He learned from his mother that she miscarried before and after his own birth, and he thought that in consequence he was regarded as both special and fragile. The crisis for him came when he was four years old and a younger sister was born. In his eyes, his sister was the preferred child. His sense of being displaced was marked for him in a particularly vivid way. He remembered his mother returning home from hospital with the baby girl in her arms, and his being sent away for several months because he was, in his mother's words, 'out of control'. During his absence from home one incident stood out in his memory: he recalled being stung by a wasp, the sting causing a large swelling. He was taken into the children's sanatorium and given special (medical) attention.

From that time Mr Jackson never really considered himself part of the family. His achievements at school and in his professional life had the effect of further alienating him from home and from his roots. The price he paid for his success was an increasing sense of loneliness and a feeling he belonged nowhere. This discomfort remained with him and connected with an uneasy suspicion that there was something intrinsically wrong with him, so accounting for his sense of not being 'at home' with others.

In contrast with her husband, Mrs Jackson was a rounded but trim woman of thirty-one. Behind her forthright manner was a shrewd watchfulness. She described the problem as belonging to her husband, and said that if he were less persistently critical and undermining, life would be bearable. As things stood, however, she was giving serious thought to leaving him.

Like her husband, Mrs Jackson came from a working-class background, although, unlike his parents, hers were strict orthodox Jews. In her view, her father's way of caring for the family was primarily by earning money. He did two jobs which meant that he was seldom available to his wife or the children, of whom there were four. Being the only girl, Mrs Jackson tended to be used by her mother as confidante and ally in bringing up the family. She thought this probably moulded the way she was regarded by her family and others in later life. Having coped at home, she thought others now saw her as the competent, managing type. She lamented that this failed to take account of another side of her and said how bitterly angry she sometimes felt about having, as she saw it, foregone her childhood.

In some respects, Mrs Jackson considered herself to have been uncomfortably intertwined in her parents' marriage. There was a sense of illicit excitement and repulsion at being privy to some intimate aspects of their relationship. Her room had adjoined her parents' bedroom and she remembered hearing their lovemaking at night. Sometimes her mother would confide to her the next morning that her father had been 'at it again'. This experience at home was relevant to Mrs Jackson's stated reasons for her reluctance to have intercourse with her husband. Rose slept in the bedroom adjoining their own and would often come into their room in the early morning, the time Mr Jackson was most likely to want to make love. Mrs Jackson became aware that she was attributing to Rose the feelings that she herself had experienced as a child, and this inhibited her sexual responsiveness.

Besides herself, there were three other children in the family, all boys. Her elder brother was boarded out for reasons which were unclear, except that he was regarded as the boy 'whom nobody could do anything with'. The next boy was two years younger than Mrs Jackson. Because he was often ill and suffered from asthma he was regarded as the frail member of the family who needed special care. Mrs Jackson felt she lost her mother to this brother. Eight years junior to him was the youngest boy. He was enjoyed by the family for his resilience, particularly in standing up to his father, and he carried many of the family's hopes. That the youngest but toughest member of the family should die suddenly at the age of fifteen was a devastating blow. Mrs Jackson remembered how collapsed the family was immediately afterwards, and how, true to form, she had coped with the funeral arrangements and seen everyone through. It was only later that she herself 'collapsed' with an illness which her doctor described as delayed grief-reaction.

Mrs Jackson considered her family experience to have been turbulent. The Jewish culture, along with the need to support a hard-working father and an ailing brother, had the effect of placing men first in the pecking order, and this she resented. Since teenage years she had suffered from an irritable colon which she thought was connected with tension and her tendency to hide her feelings. When asked why it had to be that way, she replied that otherwise it would be like 'riding a roller coaster', which she associated with feeling quite out of control.

The marriage

Mr and Mrs Jackson met at a party. Mrs Jackson recalled that she had been talking to friends when he joined their group, interrupting what she was saying and taking no notice when she tried to put him down. At the time, she was not impressed by him, but he kept telephoning and pursuing her in a way she found irresistible. In retrospect, she thought it was important that she could not ride roughshod over him as she had tended to do with other 'lame duck' boyfriends. She felt it was important for each of them that the other would not 'give in'. She remembered a girlfriend telling her she would marry Mr Jackson because he was the first man she had said she must consult before accepting an invitation on his behalf as well as her own.

Mr Jackson said he liked and was physically attracted to his wife when they met. She was slimmer then; in fact she was not well. During the early months of their courtship she was admitted to hospital for the removal of fibroids, which she described as 'tumours'. There were post-operative complications which aggravated her irritable colon, and she remembered being told that a baby would put all that right. Mr Jackson remembered thinking that she might have cancer and die. While the thought frightened him, it also aroused a note of romantic attachment to the idea of a youthful tragedy in which he was separated from the object of his love. His concern for her 'swellings' was at this stage benign.

Much of the Jacksons' courtship was conducted at a distance, he working in London while she attended a course in the north of England. They saw each other at weekends, and Mrs Jackson increasingly felt torn between her attachment to Mr Jackson and her commitment to the course and her career. After six months she suggested they end their relationship so that she could get on with her studies. This prompted Mr Jackson to propose marriage, and Mrs Jackson gave up her training for him. They were married for nearly three years before Rose was born.

Comment

Mr and Mrs Jackson's early relationship followed a pattern different both from the one previously established in their respective families, and from when Rose was born and they had a family of their own. What seemed to have been important to Mrs Jackson was that she had found a man in whom she saw a robustness and capacity to withstand her which promised a chance of recovering some of the care and attention for herself which she felt she had foregone in childhood. Similarly, Mr Jackson was attracted to a woman who was not immediately accessible, but who in the end chose him in preference to her career. Moreover, for Mr Jackson, their courtship was tinged with the prospect of loss, either through death or through desertion of him for studies, which echoed painful aspects of a past separation. These hopes and associations were not, of course, the only basis for their relationship, but they demonstrate an important connection between the past and the present which during courtship raised the possibility that the course of history for each partner might be changed for the better. This hope can be expressed for each of them as the growing awareness of a possibility that their foregone childhood might be recovered. Mr Jackson might recover the exclusive attention which had been lost when his sister was born; Mrs Jackson might recover in herself the 'child' to whom she related so competently in others. Perhaps the determination that things should be different was enshrined in Mrs Jackson's decision to marry outside the synagogue, a significant gesture from a girl of orthodox parentage.

Because loss was an experience the Jacksons had in common, the birth of Rose alienated each parent from the other, and, in a sense, recreated their pasts. At one level, Mr Jackson's attack on his wife's belly can be related to his feelings about losing his mother to a younger sister. Rose then stood for the sister who displaced him, and Mrs Jackson for the mother who 'abandoned' him. For Mrs Jackson, the ailing and self-preoccupied behaviour of her husband, in addition to Rose's demands, stirred feelings about an asthmatic brother who needed caring for at her expense. The hopes during courtship receded to a honeymoon memory; once again they were faced with the painful feelings and conflicts of their own childhood.

The view adopted here is that these feelings became unmanageable because the Jacksons viewed the present in the light of their past experience. Whatever the full reasons for his separation from home when his sister was born, to Mr Jackson it was the consequence of becoming 'out of control'. A reasonable assumption, which was subsequently confirmed, was that his mother's description, as he recalled it, related to the emotional intensity of his reactions to the birth of a younger sister. An association formed in his mind between experiencing such feelings and consequent banishment. It is likely that the child's interpretation of this separation from home would at one level have been in terms of punishment for being bad—in this context, for being 'out of control'. The wasp sting was like a marker incident symbolising punishment for badness and pain resulting from displacement and separation. The swelling was symbolic of the first stirrings of a compensatory device to secure alternative care and attention for himself.

Throughout his adult life, Mr Jackson suffered from a fear of becoming ill. When Rose was two years old these fears were specifically asssociated with cancer. He would worry over ulcers in his mouth and swollen glands in his neck. He would believe that other areas of his body had developed malignant lumps and he frequently sought medical reassurance. His fears about his health became intense and specific at the time he stood down from local political work, which had previously given him considerable kudos. From being heavily committed, he had time on his hands and felt like a displaced person in changed surroundings.

Rose's birth heralded for Mr Jackson a period of renewed concern about swellings; he criticised his wife's figure, he worried in case his daughter's head was abnormally large, and he searched his own body for signs of cancer. Cancer became the symbol for unacceptable feelings which threatened to control and destroy him if he could not master them. Such 'badness' could be in him, or it could be in others. There were striking connections between the cancerous swelling he feared discovering in himself, the abnormally swollen head he imagined his daughter to have, the swollen belly that he attacked in his wife, the swollen belly of his mother during pregnancy, and the swelling resulting from the wasp sting of earlier years. The significance of these swellings for both partners of the marriage provided a therapeutic focus during the time they attended the Institute for help, and is elaborated upon in Appendix II.

A CRISIS OF SEPARATENESS

Both the Grants and the Jacksons would have appeared as unexceptional young parents to the outside observer. They held responsible professional jobs, and to their colleagues and friends relatively little of their disturbance would have been evident. Their experiences of starting a family may seem extreme when subjected to the scrutiny of examination, but they will bear comparison with the ill-defined inner stirrings of many couples who have to cope with the responsibilities of parenthood for the first time, and with the results of some research findings relating to parents who have not sought professional help for themselves.

For both couples, the birth of a baby reactivated past conflicts and made demands of them as parents which temporarily overtaxed their capacity to contain the resulting tension. It was as if marriage, as a container, had succeeded in bringing to life, in the form of a real child, the child each parent hoped to realise in themselves. As it turned out, the experience temporarily frustrated rather than fulfilled that hope. Their crisis was related to a separateness in marriage which followed the arrival of a third person in the family. It was an unmanageable experience because it compounded memories of past separations. In both cases, the attempt to manage the tensions which ensued, for example by one or other parent becoming over-involved with the child, was at the expense of the marriage. Yet security in the marriage was necessary for the creative involvement of the parents with their children.

In both cases, the crisis for the marriage came not when the baby was born, but when the child was becoming, in Mr Grant's words, 'a little aware of herself as a person'. The threesome was then properly established. It may have been that, for each couple, the toddler's first steps away from parents under-lined the crisis of separateness which the parents were experiencing in their partnership. How realistic it was to argue from clinical experience that change in marriage is registered by couples later, rather than earlier, in parenthood, was unclear at this stage. We suspected that the timing of, and vulnerability to crises were capable of a wide degree of variation, according to differing circumstances and the singular meaning of events when interpreted in the light of individual experience. It did, however, raise the important question of *when* couples were likely to be most receptive to programmes of preparation for parenthood.

As well as raising a question about the timing of intervention during important moments of change in people's lives, the experience of the Grants and the Jacksons created an interest in what preparation might mean when the outcome of change is not foreseeable. Before proceeding to consider these, and other questions, it was important to discover whether or not their experiences were atypical, and whether there were indications in the research literature of stress amongst those who did not seek outside help.

CHAPTER TWO

Research Views

'Has the baby affected your relationship?'

'Well, you say no and I say yes, or I'll say no and you say yes and we'll scream at each other. Maybe I ought to go up the shop and get some cigarettes while you answer that question and then you can go while I do. I'm not sure that either of us will give an honest answer.'

Ann Oakley

PARTIALITY IN RESEARCH

If it is difficult for couples to assess and agree upon the extent to which a baby affects marriage, the task has been no less difficult for professional observers of family life. In attempting to go further and account for changes which are discernible, researchers have demonstrated that a wide range of different views can be supported by the same field of investigation.

Researchers, in common with the couples they observe, are restricted in what they can see. There is in the nature of scientific enquiry an element of partiality. To study in detail is to narrow the field of vision; to select one area for investigation is to ignore another. In so far as different fields of study are inter-related, an area designated for investigation is, if not 'the creation of the investigator' (Minuchin, 1974), an artefact, in the sense that it has been segregated from the wider context of which it is a part. Moreover, some areas are commended or cry out for investigation more than others. Their appeal, or the appeal of their protagonists, must resonate with the investigator if his attention is to be engaged. In a non-pejorative sense, it is true to say that the researcher has an interest in, and is a partial observer of, his field of study.

One important purpose of social research is to inform action, whether at the level of policy-making or that of individual professional practice. To inform action, the researcher's material must be interpreted, and for this he will rely upon his professional frame of reference. Here a different constraint comes into play. While the interpretation provides a key to action, the same phenomenon may be capable of upholding different interpretations which, in turn, may suggest different courses of action. For example, the study of post-natal depression, perhaps the most celebrated of parental 'conditions', has prompted endocrinologists to look to metabolic systems, psychologists to psychic systems, and sociologists to social systems for both information and explanation. It is by no means clear that any one approach will be able to provide 'an honest answer', in the sense of the whole truth. The most that can be hoped for is that different contributions will not 'scream at each other', but will add to our understanding of a complex whole.

The research studies drawn upon in this chapter were carried out in England, America and Western Europe over the past twenty-five years. They apply to a period during which, in these societies, there have been significant changes in the relationships between the sexes, and in the institution of marriage. The microcosmic study of family change has taken place against a background of wider social change. In this general climate of uncertainty, the specific uncertainties associated with family transitions assume special significance.

When considering the changes brought about by parenthood, many studies have concentrated primarily upon the relationship between a mother and her baby. Fathers, when mentioned, have often been regarded as peripheral to the central family drama. To the extent that the emphasis has changed in recent studies, it is possible to infer a change in social values. For example, there has been a reaction against the notion that parenthood means motherhood (Rutter, 1974), a movement away from exclusively child-centred values (Rapoport *et al.*, 1977), and a swing from segregated role relationships towards more shared involvement in contemporary expectations of marriage (HO/DHSS, 1979). In the place of essentially insular values (in the sense that they focus upon the interests and responsibilities of individuals in isolation from others with whom they interact), there is an emerging awareness of the importance of partnerships, and particularly the marital partnership, in effectively carrying out family responsibilities and promoting the well-being of family members.

This chapter will concentrate upon research studies which have added to our understanding of the mutual influence exerted by children upon marriage, and by the marital partnership upon its offspring. Particular attention will be paid to the implications of the birth of a first baby in this context. The evidence suggests that the ability to parent is significantly affected by the nature of a couple's marriage, and that marriage itself is importantly affected by parenthood.

THE EFFECT OF CHILDREN UPON MARRIAGE

Research into the effects of children upon marriage has tried to ascertain how marital stability and levels of marital satisfaction are affected by children, and to estimate and explain the degree of stress experienced by couples when they become parents for the first time. The most extreme indicator of marital stress is the breakdown of the partnership, and this provides a starting point for a review of some research findings.

Children and marital stability

In both Britain and America, the past twenty-five years have seen a steady decline in marital stability. The divorce rate in England and Wales is now six times greater than it was twenty years ago (CSO, 1982), the most dramatic increase taking place in the 1970s. Changes in matrimonial and divorce law (particularly the 1969 Divorce Reform Act) have made divorce easier to obtain and less expensive than before. However, there is no certain way of knowing whether the upward trend in divorce simply means that we are now seeing what was previously obscured by a legislative veil, or that there has been an increase in marital unhappiness, or disaffection with marriage as an institution. The divorce trend has been accompanied by a rapid increase in the number of one-parent families, with consequent implications for society which have warranted the attention of a government enquiry (Finer, 1974).

The situation in America is comparable. There, the divorce rate has doubled in the past ten years and in 1974 there was one divorce for every 2.75 marriages. In 1978 37 percent of families were estimated to have only one adult member (Daniels and Smith, 1979)

Despite the downward trend in marital stability, there are few indications in the United Kingdom of marriage becoming any less popular. Indeed, expectations of marriage seem to be higher today than ever before. Commenting upon the situation, a recent Working Party on marriage guidance concluded that:

> Our evidence and experience confirm the thesis that personal development and satisfaction are core values underlying contemporary expectations of marriage. (HO/DHSS, 1979)

It is therefore against a background of changing attitudes towards marriage, divorce and the organisation of family life that the effect of children upon marital stability must be viewed.

From the figures available, there is no evidence to suggest that children are directly responsible for their parents' divorce. Indeed, first impressions of the divorce statistics suggest that divorcing couples are relatively infertile (Thornes and Collard, 1979), although these authors advise caution in drawing any conclusions from this. One study suggests there is a U-shaped relationship between family size and dissolution rates in marriage, the latter being highest when there are no children, or, conversely, when there are many children of the marriage (Thornton, 1977). Reasons advanced for this pattern include the possibility that children defer the decision to divorce in unsatisfying marriages, but when there are many of them may tax a partnership beyond its capacity.

There is evidence to suggest that pre-marital pregnancy and the conception of a child soon after marriage are predisposing factors towards the subsequent breakdown of a marriage (Rutter and Madge, 1976; Thornes and Collard, 1979) and if not breakdown, towards considerable stress in the marital partnership (Shereshefsky and Yarrow, 1973). One study, using the National Child Development Cohort as source, found that 42.2 percent of divorced parents had conceived their first child out of wedlock and a further 28.4 percent had produced a baby within the first two years of marriage (Whitehead, 1976).

These findings lend weight to a developmental view of marriage and family life in which the ability to function appropriately at one stage of development is seen as depending upon the successful management of previous stages.

For individuals, this approach is well-established. The psycho-analytic view of individual development has paid close attention to the stages through which infants and children must pass in their journey towards competent adulthood, and they have drawn attention to the opportunities for reworking unresolved aspects of past experience in present day relationships. This approach has been taken further by Levinson (1978) and Sheehy (1977) who emphasise that adulthood has its own developmental stages, separate and distinguishable from those of childhood.

In Levinson's terminology, the birth of a first child is a significant 'marker event' in an adult's development, which has the potential to draw one era to its close and usher in the next. Sheehy adds that such events do not necessarily herald a period of development; marriage can be a flight from parental conflict, parenthood a flight from marital intimacy. In common with psycho-analytic work, these studies give pride of place to the quest of men and women for a viable identity, one capable of change while maintaining a continuity over time, to cope with tasks and responsibilities appropriate to different phases of development.

Applied to marriage and the family, the developmental view implies that social groups must similarly evolve a flexible identity if they are to function well and constituent members are to be properly served. Social scientists have accordingly described families as 'transitional systems of social roles' (Rollins and Galligan, 1978), or as:

> . . . a changing group of individuals who together in their interacting roles constitute an open system which has three primary tasks, each predominant at a different stage in the family life cycle, 'coming together', 'giving birth and forming something new', and 'drawing apart'. (Bain, 1978)

This particular definition of the family's evolving function describes very well what has been observed about marriage when a first baby is born. 'Birth unites and maternal responsibility divides,' asserts Oakley (1979), commenting upon the disillusionment of mothers in her sample. Shereshefsky and Yarrow (1973) describe the variations in marital adaptation over time in these terms:

> During pregnancy the husband-wife relationship improved, the pregnancy apparently drawing the couples closer in feeling. In the post-natal period, the relationship

deteriorated in a substantial proportion of the families, doubtless due to the strain of trying to adapt to the infant's needs and to the unfamiliar role of mother and father.

In more positive vein, Breen (1975) observed that one criterion for successful adaptation to motherhood was the capacity of parents to tolerate differentiation in their partnership after birth.

According to a developmental frame of reference, the capacity to be flexible depends in large measure upon previous experience. Dumon (1978), in reviewing this approach, identifies as its most significant feature the central assumption that each stage in the family life cycle is not only preceded by, but prepared for and to some extent pre-determined by preceding phases:

> The process indicated by 'when two become three', is not a mere product or the sole effect of an event (childbirth), but the result of situations and relations in preceding phases. It is an historic momentum.

The importance of establishing a marriage before taking on parental responsibilities is strongly indicated by such an approach. One explanation for the statistical association between marital breakdown and pre-marital pregnancy and conception early on in marriage can be in terms of a failure to establish the marriage, and a fusion of different developmental stages which leads to behaviour inappropriate to chronological age.

'Establishing the marriage' is, however, an ambiguous task, and not necessarily achieved by delaying the advent of children. La Rossa (1977) has demonstrated that the decision to start a family can be rooted in the power politics of a marriage. Its potential significance is manifold—to demonstrate love, to end a disagreement, to save a marriage, to provide a common interest, to tie a husband down or to increase distance in the partnership. The child can be the symbol of both unity and disunity, of having established or having failed to establish a marriage. Add to this the unconscious significance of parenthood (which was discussed in the previous chapter) and the problems of reconciling a developmental view of family life with a general strategy of preventive intervention become apparent.

The developmental view of marriage has evolved in part from studies considering changes in marital satisfaction brought about by children. Changes in levels of satisfaction are more commonly experienced than marital breakdown, and it is to this area that attention will now turn.

Children and marital satisfaction

The past twenty years have produced a body of evidence, from America in particular, suggesting that marital satisfaction is adversely affected by the arrival of children (Blood and Wolfe, 1960; Bradburn and Caplovitz, 1965; Burr, 1970; Rollins and Feldman, 1970; Ryder, 1973; Rollins and Cannon, 1974; Lerner and Spanier, 1978). In the United Kingdom, a study of working-class women with children at home found that four in ten of the sample experienced either considerable dissatisfaction with their marriage or noticeably little warmth and enthusiasm about it (Brown and Harris, 1978). Whether children are directly responsible, or other factors play their part (like the 'corrosion of time' commented upon by Blood and Wolfe) has not always been clear.

The American studies have detected a weak U-shape relationship between levels of marital satisfaction and the child-rearing years. According to these studies the sharpest drop in satisfaction occurs in the pre-school years, but it is not until children leave home that satisfaction from the marriage is likely to regain something of its former level. Some studies refine the U-shape association into a W, identifying the point at which the last child starts school and the adolescent years as particular troughs within the general dip. However, the evidence is not clear cut. One study suggests that children provide alternative sources of satisfaction (Luckey and Bain, 1970), while another indicates that some couples derive more satisfaction from their marriage with the arrival of children (Feldman, 1971).

In connection with this last point, Feldman explained the difference between couples who were more satisfied with their marriage once they had children and those who were less satisfied, in terms of there being an inverse relationship between levels of satisfaction and the degree of role segregation in a marriage. Couples who shared many interests and derived a high degree of satisfaction from combined activities he described as having 'companionate marriages'. Those who derived satisfaction primarily from activities and relationships outside the marriage, and whose roles were separately defined, he described as having 'differentiated marriages'. By definition, differentiated couples derived less satisfaction from their marriage than companionate couples. Working on the assumption that the birth of a baby increases the need for co-operation and involvement between parents, Feldman suggested that differentiated couples might well derive more satisfaction from marriage than before. Conversely, since parenthood increases role segregation in a marriage, there is, in some respects, a crisis of difference for companionate relationships, which in their case accounts for a decline in levels of marital satisfaction.

This observation is particularly interesting when set against a social climate in which there is assumed to be less differentiation between the sexes, and in which marriage is often perceived primarily as a companionate relationship. Here may be found one explanation for the suggestion that children have a depressing effect upon levels of marital satisfaction. Such an explanation does, however, need to be counterbalanced by studies which indicate a high degree of role segregation in marriage today (Oakley, 1974; Edgell, 1980; Leonard, 1980).

Studies concerned with the effect of children upon marital satisfaction have generally covered the whole of the child-rearing lifecycle. There are other studies which have confined themselves to the examination of transitional stress associated with first time parenthood.

Transitional stress associated with parenthood

These studies can be divided into three categories: those which address themselves to the family as a unit, those concerned with the effect of motherhood upon women, and those concerned with the effect of fatherhood upon men.

(*a*) *From two to three*

What have become known as the 'Transition to Parenthood' studies have differed in their assessment of the degree of stress involved in becoming a parent, and by implication, therefore, of the consequent degree of stress upon marriage.

The debate opened with the publication of a study which reported that 83 per cent of an urban middle-class sample of American couples experienced parenthood as a severe or extensive crisis in their lives (Le Masters, 1957). Crisis was defined in terms of a sharp decisive change for which existing ways of managing were found wanting. Wives complained of chronic tiredness, extensive confinement at home, the curtailment of social life, long waking hours, a decline in housekeeping standards, and worry about themselves and their appearance. Husbands echoed these themes adding their disillusionment with parenthood, their sense of greater financial pressure, and their concern about a decline in sexual responsiveness from their wives. Le Masters commented that:

> . . . listening to them describe their experiences, one felt that these young parents could be compared to veterans of military service; they had been through a rough experience but it was worth it.

He concluded that:

> the arrival of the first child forces young married couples to take the last painful step into the adult world.

Dyer (1963) confirmed this impression of parenthood as a critical event in adult life.

Sifting through research findings it is possible to build up a gloomy impression of early family life—certainly one which is at odds with the picture sometimes presented by the media. There is, for example, evidence of increased marital violence during pregnancy (Gelles, 1975), of sexual infidelity around the period of confinement (Curtis, 1955; Masters and Johnson, 1966; Lacousiere, 1972; Shereshefsky and Yarrow, 1973), and of a temporary deterioration in sexual relationships after birth (Landis *et al.*, 1952; Hamilton, 1962; Meyerowitz and Feldman, 1966; Frommer and O'Shea, 1973b;

Udenberg, 1974; Oakley, 1979b). One English study found that 13 per cent of a group of mothers who were separated from their parents before the age of eleven were also separated from their husbands one year after their baby was born, and a further 22 per cent were experiencing strain in their marriage (Frommer and O'Shea, 1973a). Another recorded that 73 per cent of a sample of mothers interviewed when their babies were five months old reported a decline in marital happiness (Oakley, 1979b).

That, clearly, is not the whole story. Other studies have highlighted the satisfying aspects of becoming a parent and have repudiated the notion that 'every butterfly is a frustrated caterpillar', to use a phrase of Marris (1974). In America, several studies have refuted the suggestion that the experience of becoming a parent amounts to a crisis for most people, reporting that while there are 'bothersome' aspects, most couples who want a child find the experience rewarding (Hobbs, 1965, 1968; Jacoby, 1969; Falicov, 1971; Russell, 1974; Hobbs and Cole, 1976; Hobbs and Wimbish, 1977). Accordingly, there has been a linguistic swing away from the word 'crisis' towards the word 'transition' to describe the nature of the experience of becoming a parent (for example, Parkes, 1971, 1979).

The significance of these studies lies in their suggestion that if expectations can be realigned with what is known about likely reactions to parenthood, the degree of transitional stress will be reduced. The movement favouring programmes of education for parenthood derives support from them.

The capacity of a marriage successfully to accommodate a third person in the family is affected by the ability of the parties to come to terms with changes in their role and status. The transition from wife to mother, or husband to father, is an integral part of the transition from two to three. The person who comes across as most vulnerable in this process is the woman.

(b) From wife to mother

The experience of becoming a mother in the United Kingdom seems likely to involve some measure of depression. One study estimated that one in four working-class first-time mothers became depressed during pregnancy, and 14 per cent seriously enough to impair their lives and relationships (Zacijek and Wolkind, 1978). Far more common is the experience of post-natal depression, although what is meant by the term, and the range of experience it describes, is not as clear-cut as might be thought from a first glance.

Oakley (1979a) refers to five categories of post-natal depression. At the extreme ends of the spectrum are the 'blues' and post-puerperal psychosis. The 'blues' refer to a tendency towards tearfulness and a vulnerability to upset which occurs within the first week or so after birth. In her sample, 84 per cent of mothers experienced such feelings. Other studies put the range between 68 per cent (Pitt, 1973) and 80 per cent (Robin, 1962; Breen, 1975). Post-

puerperal psychosis, as the name implies, describes a much more serious condition requiring psychiatric treatment. Its occurrence is rare; about three in every
thousand mothers will experience it (Breen, 1975).

Between these extremes come three intermediate stages of depression. The first
covers a mother's feelings of tenseness, anxiety and ultra-sensitivity upon first
coming home from hospital with her baby. Oakley (1979a) reported that 71 per
cent of her sample had these reactions. The transition from hospital to home is
virtually unavoidable because of the almost complete absence of services
facilitating domiciliary confinements for first-time mothers. The second stage
covers the early weeks and months after birth; 33 per cent of her sample suffered
depressed moods during this period. Finally, there are those with 'clinical'
depression, a constant state including appetite disturbance, insomnia and panic
attacks. Oakley included 24 per cent of her sample in this category. Pitt (1968)
found 10.8 per cent of his sample of mothers were depressed. Frommer and
O'Shea (1973b) recorded that, one year after giving birth, 64 per cent of wives
who had been separated from their parents before the age of eleven were showing
such depressed symptoms as were 34 per cent of their control group. Brown and
Harris (1978) found evidence of definite psychiatric disturbance in 31 per cent of
their sample of London working-class mothers with children under six years old.
In an earlier paper (Brown *et al.*, 1975), Brown cites a North London study which
reported that 41 per cent of young mothers showed signs of depression. Richman
(1974, 1976) has also made references to the extent of depression amongst
mothers with young children, associating this primarily with housing difficulties.

In an attempt to account for this depression—if not actual deterioration in personality (Rossi, 1968)—and the variations in ability to adapt to motherhood, three
broad explanations have been offered. The first points to hormonal changes taking
place during pregnancy and immediately after birth (Hamilton, 1962; Dalton,
1971). For example, immediately after birth there is a drop in the progesterone
level following the discharge of the placenta, and this can have an effect upon
mood. Oakley (1979a) has criticised this explanation on the grounds that it fails to
account for depression during pregnancy, or for long term depression, although it
has been applied to both. Work done by Gelder (1978) suggests that evidence for
an endocrinological explanation of post-natal depression is, as yet, inconclusive.
He adds that it is most likely to have relevance in connection with the 'blues', a
view reinforced by work done in Australia (reported by Watson, 1977).

A second explanation has been offered in psychological terms. These writers
stress the intrapsychic nature of the experience of becoming a mother. For
example:

A first pregnancy, despite its social ramifications and interpersonal meaning, appears
from our results to be essentially an intrapsychic experience, one in which the woman is
responding less to significant persons and events in her life than to immediate physiological and emotional developments from within (Shereshefsky and Yarrow, 1973).

Similarly, Winnicott (1956) and Chertok (1969) draw attention to the pre-occupation of mothers with themselves and their infants in the early post-partum months before re-emerging into the wider social world.

While the experience may be seen as predominantly intra-psychic, many writers (for example, Gordon, 1965; Pitt, 1968; Zacijek and Wolkind, 1978), suggest that pregnancy and motherhood are not of themselves sufficient conditions to account for depression; in their view there have to be additional pre-disposing psychiatric factors. These studies, in so far as they correlate depression with descriptions of personality states, are unsatisfying to the extent that they see personalities as fixed variables, relatively unaffected by social and temporal factors. They tend to give little insight into why people are as they are at particular times in their lives.

The most helpful psychological contributions have paid attention to a mother's perception of her relationship with her own mother as a central feature of her capacity to reconcile herself with motherhood. It is as if a woman's secure internalised relationship with her own mother can act in much the same way as an external support, making the actual presence of others less necessary because of this internal resource upon which she can draw. If she feels that her 'internal mother' is absent (Frommer and O'Shea, 1973a), or com-petitive (Deutsch, 1944, 1945), or undermining and controlling (Bibring, 1959; Chertok et al., 1969), she will be less likely to derive support from this source and she may have difficulty in reconciling herself to her private perception of what it means to be a mother. This difficulty is often particularly acute because characteristics ascribed to an 'internal mother' are likely to include aspects of a woman's own personality which she is at pains to blot out, but which have 'come home to roost', so to speak, by virtue of her pregnancy and her self-admission to motherhood.

What it means to be a 'good enough' mother has received particular atten-tion from Winnicott, and he has written about this in a way which can be readily understood by parents themselves (Winnicott, 1964). He incorporates acceptable levels of parental failure as an essential part of a child's experience if, in later life, he or she is not to be excessively self-critical or demanding. Breen's (1975) study of first-time mothers is interesting in that 38 per cent of her sample who had difficulty adjusting to motherhood were also reported to have a poor identification with their own mothers, a low degree of self-confi-dence, little change in the way they perceived themselves before and after birth, and a preoccupation with idealised impressions of motherhood. About this last point she comments:

> This image of the all-sacrificing mother is a cultural one, but it is also one which results from a very primitive psychological mechanism involving the separation of good and bad qualities which are then ascribed to different people—the fairies and witches of childhood (it is the process called 'splitting').

She goes on to conclude that:

> . . . those women who are most adjusted to childbearing are those who are less en-
> slaved by the experience, have more differentiated, more open appraisals of them-
> selves and other people, do not aspire to be the perfect, selfless mother which they
> might have felt their own mother had not been but are able to call on a good mother
> image with which they can identify, and do not experience themselves as passive, the
> cultural stereotype of femininity.

The concept of maternal role is, from a psychological point of view, a highly
idiosyncratic one which refers to a woman's perception of her past relationship
with her own mother. The psychological approach has, however, been criticised
for paying too much attention to the significance of 'rejecting the feminine
role' (Oakley, 1979a) and too little to social factors. It is to this third area that
we now turn.

In the United Kingdom, the work of Brown and others (1975, 1978) and
Oakley (1979a, 1979b, 1980), has proposed that depression amongst young
mothers can be understood in terms of their social environment. Brown found
no evidence to suggest that life events were of themselves responsible for
maternal depression, but only in conjunction with pre-disposing factors like
poor housing, an unsupportive marriage, unemployment and financial difficulties. He found that among parents with children at home, working-class
mothers were four times more likely than their middle-class counterparts to
suffer from a definite psychiatric disorder because they were more likely to have
to contend with difficult circumstances and were less protected against them.
He identified women particularly at risk as those who had three or more
children under the age of fourteen at home, who had lost their own mother
under the age of eleven and who did not have an intimate tie (in which he
included as important a supportive marriage or co-habiting relationship). The
significance of a secure marriage in alleviating adaptive stress has been
remarked upon by other researchers (Deutsch, 1945, Gordon *et al.*, 1960,
1965; Douglas, 1968; Russell, 1974).

Brown draws attention to the significance of the experience of loss in explaining depression. In our culture, motherhood usually involves giving up work
and therefore the social network and sense of identity provided by employment. Thirty years ago this change would have coincided with marriage; now it
coincides with parenthood, an event which itself demands an important
reworking of personal identity. There is a loss of intimacy in marriage, a loss of
space at home, a loss of time for oneself and a loss of financial and physical
resources to cope with the demands of a baby. Moreover, there is usually a loss
of what has not been realised—the hopes, ideas and expectations about parenthood which have not been fulfilled by experience.

The extent of disillusionment among mothers is noted by Oakley (1979b). In her sample of middle class London women, 82 per cent said their experience of pregnancy was not what they had expected, 93 per cent said the same about birth, and 90 per cent said their picture of motherhood changed with the experience. Reality usually proved to be less inviting than fantasy, and this often affected the self-esteem of the women concerned. By the time their babies were five months old, one third of her sample had returned to work, if only to part-time employment.

Oakley pays particular attention to the initiation of women into motherhood and is critical of what she calls the 'colonization of birth by medicine' (1979b). She found evidence of an association between high technology births (particularly instrumental deliveries and epidural analgesia) and the 'blues'. The general drift to what has been called the 'medicalisation' of life has been commented upon by other writers (Brearley et al., 1978) and Oakley's figures for technical intervention in the deliveries of her sample of sixty-six women are arresting: 79 per cent had epidural anaesthetics and only one mother had no pain-killing drugs; 41 per cent were induced; 52 per cent had forceps or ventouse deliveries and 98 per cent had episiotomies. Macfarlane (1977) supports the association between technological intervention at birth and depression, and compares the rate of drug relief in Britain (80 per cent) adversely with countries like Holland (5 per cent) and Sweden (12 per cent) who have lower perinatal mortality rates than our own (Klosterman, 1976). Cartwright (1975) suggests that the point of diminishing returns has been reached when hospital confinements can increase from 64 per cent of births in 1959 to 96 per cent in 1974, inductions from 15 per cent in 1965 to 41 per cent in 1974, and caesarian deliveries from 2.7 per cent in 1958 to 4.5 per cent in 1970 with virtually no change in perinatal mortality rates.

The greater the technical intervention, the less likely a woman is to feel she has control over her own body. While medical care can contribute towards the physical safety of both mother and child, the evidence suggests that there is a psychological cost attached to present medical practice. The experience of helplessness has been associated with depression in behavioural studies (Seligman, 1975) and it is likely to be particularly disabling when it immediately precedes the magnitude of parental responsibility which a mother must assume upon her return home from hospital. Some hospitals are well aware of the problem and are investigating ways in which the disabling aspects of hospital confinement can be reduced.

Oakley asserts that post-natal depression can be accounted for solely in terms of social factors and the medical management of childbirth, and one might add that her conclusions are supported by work which suggests that in our culture the definition of sexual roles has laid an undue burden upon women to carry and express the weight of feelings in heterosexual partnerships (Hinchcliffe et al., 1978). She suggests that it is less the women who need to adjust to motherhood, than social and medical institutions which need to adjust to the needs of mothers. This wider view was heralded by the work of Gavron (1968) who, in commenting upon the depressed status of women in Western society, wrote:

> There is an air of confusion which hangs over the whole question of women and their functions in society which seems at times to extend to every aspect of their activities . . . what is needed above all is some deliberate attempt to reintegrate women in all their many roles with the central activities of society.

(c) From husband to father

If there is uncertainty about the role of mothers in society, the same can be said about fathers—especially during pregnancy, birth and the early months of parenthood. However, less has been written about their predicament.

Research referred to earlier suggested that during pregnancy, marital partnerships tend to become closer and less differentiated than before. The baby brings more need for separateness and segregation in conjugal roles. In some primitive societies this segregation has been ameliorated by the practice of the 'couvade' (from the French 'couver', to brood, incubate or hatch). Anthropologists have used the term to describe socially prescribed practices carried out by fathers in preparation for birth and their subsequent change in role and status. Many practices resemble pregnancy or labour. Mead (1962) noted that the Arapesh Indians, a tribe which valued maternal qualities in men and where both parents were actively involved with their children, practised rituals in which the men observed their wives' pregnancy taboos and shared their childbirth bed. Similarly, Mohave Indian men were ceremonially de-livered of stones when their wives were giving birth. While these rituals marked a social transition for the men (Rapoport and Rapoport, 1968) they may also have had the psychic function of managing feelings of envy in connection with the manifest creativity of women, the more so in a community where sexual roles were not greatly differentiated.

In Western society, the experience, and perhaps even ritualisation, of the couvade is less conscious. Curtis (1955) observed that from a sample of expectant fathers in the US armed forces, 65 per cent developed pregnancy symptoms without connecting their symptoms with their wives' condition. The symptoms included tiredness, nausea, backache, gastro-intestinal trouble, weight-gain and toothache. Trethowan (1968) found similar symptoms in expectant fathers and Lacousiere (1972) and Richards (1980) have extended the range to include emotional disturbance. It has been suggested that affective disturbance during pregnancy can reflect male guilt at having damaged or inflicted pain upon women (Shereshefsky and Yarrow, 1973).

The ritualisation of the couvade is more obscure, although some have sug-gested it is reflected in obstetric practice during childbirth. The effect of increasing the number of hospital confinements is to bring the act of female creativity within the orbit of male control. Medical practice prescribes that while midwives can perform episiotomies (in a sense, inflict damage), their repair remains the province of the (usually male) doctor (Oakley, 1979b). One psychoanalytic interpretation of this practice is that its function is to help contain men's envy of (and therefore wish to destroy) the creativity of women. Lewis (1976) holds that obstetric practice is influenced by unconscious factors of this kind. The reparative drive may have some bearing upon why men tolerate without protest the 'entrance trauma' of going into hospital with their wives, described by Richman *et al.* (1975):

> In some ways the father's presence at birth can be likened to a small boy permitted to enter the sanctum of the school staffroom. . . . He can be dismissed at will while the doctor makes an examination. His rights to be present are not only limited but vague. . . . At the birth he is not certain what to do, where to stand or put his hands. Holding hands with his wife is more reminiscent of courtship, but the situation is now radically different. . . . Despite being gowned from head to toe he may not feel part of the delivery team. And this attire can symbolically erase the special relationship with his wife.

This may not be every father's experience of attending at birth, and hospital practice has continued to change to accommodate husbands more easily. At the same time, the analogy with the small boy is apposite when psychological aspects of male transitional stress are taken into account. Pines (1978) makes reference to how a man's feelings about relinquishing his wife to a baby can evoke the experience of an earlier triangular configuration in which, as a boy, he managed, to a greater or lesser degree, to relinquish exclusive claim over his mother for a stronger identification with father. While childhood feelings may be re-awakened by the baby, the traditional role ascribed to fathers has been that of the responsible isolate, the man who recharges his wife's batteries and holds on to her adult self so that she can become engrossed with her baby without fearing any loss of herself in consequence (Caplan, 1961; Gaddini, 1976). His ability to act in this way, in effect to mother his wife, is also affected by how at ease he feels with maternal aspects of his own personality and how prepared he is to forego his own needs (Ballou, 1978). His identity, in common with that of his wife, is under pressure at this time, and each partner may look to the other for reassurance and support at a time when neither feels in a strong position to help.

A social climate which offers no clear prescription for parental behaviour (surveyed by Bax, 1976) allows greater freedom of choice to couples in working out their roles. It also affords fewer guidelines and places a considerable burden of personal responsibility upon parents for the choices they make. There is a move towards more flexibility in the allocation of parental roles (Rapoport and Rapoport, 1971; Rapoport *et al., 1977), and the institution of paternity leave* in a growing number of firms (Karpf, 1979) suggests that parenting is increasingly being recognised as the responsibility of a partnership rather than of one person. Reviewing the shift in post-war attitudes, the Rapoports contrast the old order (in which 'there was an authoritative set of formulations . . . that idealised a conception of the nuclear conjugal family, with relatively standardised composition, division of labour and lifecycle timetable. This conception—with its expectations that "normal", "mature" men will be economic providers, "normal", "mature" women will be housewives and mothers—has been bolstered by clinical psychiatry (as in the work of Bowlby and Winnicott), medicine (as in the early work of Spock), sociology (as in the work of Parsons), and by professionals in law, education and social work. The conception has been rationalized as "natural" in the sense of biologically determined, universal amongst human societies and therefore reflecting a human imperative, adapted to our own society and therefore "functional"') with the new, which values shared parenting above unitary parenting, balanced parental sacrifice above total sacrifice and an appreciation of the joys and sorrows of parenthood above an unrealistic, idealised image of family life.

The preceding discussion suggests that the ways in which children affect marriage are both diverse and complex to ascertain. Birth is a social, psychological and physical event, and attempts to understand its significance for marriage must take account of all three dimensions. For couples, the birth of a first baby is an event of pivotal significance, which carries the prospect of change and renewal, or stagnation and decline.

THE EFFECT OF MARRIAGE UPON CHILDREN

It is a matter of commonsense that the nature of a couple's marriage will be an important influence upon their children's future wellbeing. The clinical and empirical literature supporting this contention is vast and beyond the scope of this chapter. While the infant or child is no *tabula rasa*, and actively affects the responses of those around him (Rapoport et al., 1977; Lerner and Spanier, 1978), the influence of parents upon their children is critically important to their future health and happiness. The quality of the parents' marriage has consistently been associated with the happiness, satisfaction and stability of a person's own marriage, and provides the only model of a close adult relationship which a child is likely to experience over a long period of time. In this respect it serves as a blueprint for a child's future heterosexual relationships (Rutter and Madge, 1976). Moreover, the capacity of parents to convey mutual concern, and the quality of their relationship, is likely to have a more profound influence upon a child than his individual relationship with either parent (Balint, 1972). In so far as the birth of a first baby is a moment of generational change, it is a turning point for all concerned which can influence whether past legacies are handed on unchanged to future generations or whether there is room for a creative response to the challenge of this important personal and family transition.

Because the well-being of children is intrinsically bound up with the well-being of their parents, the earlier discussion in this chapter cannot be divorced from considerations of the effect of marriage upon children. This section will be confined to research studies which have a bearing upon the issue during the relatively brief period of pregnancy, birth and the early months of life.

There is strong evidence to suggest that the physical and emotional well-being of a mother during pregnancy and after is significantly affected by marriage (Sinclair, 1975). One of the serendipitous findings of a study of women during pregnancy was reported in this way:

> . . . despite our initial assumption that successful adaptation to the intensely personal experience of pregnancy is dependent primarily on the woman's physical and mental health, our clinical impression was that an uncomplicated pregnancy depended to an even greater extent on the success of the marital relationship (Wenner et al., 1969).

This view is developed by Cohen (1966) for the post-natal period when he says that a good marriage can more than compensate for difficulties arising out of a woman's conflict with the maternal role as she perceives it. This correlation between marital adaptation and maternal adaptation was the most outstanding feature of work carried out by Shereshefsky and Yarrow (1973) who remarked that:

> . . . when characterised by mutuality, the husband-wife relationship is itself a deterrent to the development of stresses. The indication is that, through joint effort, a potentially stressful development can be confronted and the problem dealt with before the circumstance becomes crystallised into a persistent, serious stress.

Concluding his search of the literature relevant to physical and emotional problems during pregnancy, Sinclair (1975) writes:

> There seems to be strong clinical evidence that the marriage is usually the major factor in determining the woman's reactions during pregnancy and that the most important factor in this is the degree to which the husband is able to meet the woman's increased need for attention and support.

The effect of marriage upon the baby during labour and delivery is less well documented, although here, too, there is some evidence to suggest that a husband's presence during delivery can be beneficial. Macfarlane (1977) claims that this is so and that his presence adds to the enjoyment of birth for both parents and results in less pain and medication for the wife. His contribution is seen as particularly important in terms of providing an ally for the woman in an alien world. Russell (1974) and Breen (1975) have added some supporting evidence.

In the post-natal period the husband's contribution has been unequivocally associated with his wife's ability to adapt to her new role (Shereshefsky and Yarrow, 1973; Frommer and O'Shea, 1973), and with her capacity to identify and become appropriately preoccupied with their baby (Winnicott, 1956; Pines, 1978). Problems in infant management have been strongly correlated with current marital problems (Rutter and Madge, 1976) and there is a significant association between marital disharmony and child abuse (Evans *et al.*, 1972; Green *et al.*, 1974; Scott, 1974). In connection with this last point, it has been suggested that wives who fail to obtain support from their husbands or others turn to their children for care and comfort. Failing to provide this care, the child may be attacked in place of the absent parent or partner. This process has been referred to as the 'reversal of generations' (Richter, 1976).

MARRIAGE AND MEDIATION

The research reviewed in this chapter suggests that the relationship of marriage is of pivotal significance for individuals and families who are facing irreversible changes in their lives. Marriage serves to mediate between inner and outer worlds in two important respects.

In the first place, marriage as a social institution mediates between the requirements of other institutions which impinge upon the family, and the needs of individual family members as they change over time. In a period of social change this task is onerous. Not only must parents transmit cultural values from one generation to the next, but they must adapt them to a changing world (Wilson, 1961).

In this respect contemporary marriage is called upon to do more than ever before at a time when it has arguably never been supported less. Three hundred years ago the influence of the community, religion and the law provided a degree of certainty about rules of behaviour in marriage which has since been steadily eroded (Stone, 1977). Marriage as a private institution is a relatively recent phenomenon, and within the present century it was common practice for family members to share their home with servants, lodgers and apprentices. Surveying the change, Laslett (1974) comments that:

> To the extent that family privacy has increased . . . it is also likely that there has been a decrease in social control over, and social support for, a traditional definition of the performance of family roles.

This theme was echoed by Bott (1971) who contrasted the English 'pressure cooker marriage' with the support (but lack of privacy) available to the Polynesians of Tonga:

> In a small scale society a man may be able to love his mother, respect his sister, hate his father's sister and copulate with his wife. In our system he does all four with his wife.

Her thesis that segregated conjugal role relationships are associated with highly connected social networks (and conversely) has important implications for Western and transitional societies as well as for primitive communities. In the West, while parenthood increases the degree of role segregation in marriage, the extent of social and geographical mobility has scattered the network of families and friends who might otherwise have been called upon for day to day help. Only in small measure have the motor car and the telephone compensated for this change. Social and health care services have to some extent taken the place of the extended family. While in Western societies there are no common rites of passage of the kind described by Mead (1962), it may fall to an increasing extent upon these services to assist people at times of change in their lives. Since marriage is heavily relied upon for support by husband and wife, it may need to be to this partnership that such services should address themselves.

In the second place, marriage as a psychological relationship must mediate between the inner and outer worlds of couples so that they behave towards each other, and towards their children, in a way which is in keeping with their current position in the family.

The inner world of an individual derives importantly from his or her personal interpretation of past experience. Important events like the birth of a baby can re-evoke this experience and the conflicts associated with it. The potential of marriage to contain and re-work these conflicts, and thereby promote personal and family development, has been a key therapeutic assumption of writers like Pincus (1960) and Dicks (1967). With this additional perspective, the concept of parental role assumes different properties from those described by sociologists. In Richter's (1967) words, the definition of role must then include 'the total structure of the unconsciously determined expectations that parents place on a child,' and, indeed, upon each other. The organisation of role relationships therefore operates at two levels: at the level of current realities (parents have a role and responsibilities to discharge towards their children) and at the level of inner realities (parents have also been children with needs, experiences and feelings which are liable to re-surface in adult life and influence their behaviour and relationships). When marriage fails to regulate the flow between inner and outer worlds, the 'unsolved conflicts of the spouses are brought piggyback into the arena of child-rearing' (Minuchin, 1974).

It is not always possible to reduce the social and psychological pressures upon parents through direct action. In the short term at least, there will always be tensions which have to be tolerated. The positioning of marriage between private and public worlds means it is both particularly vulnerable yet well-placed to contain the tensions inherent in any process of change and so to increase the tolerance of those concerned. For this reason, services available during the period of change heralded by birth need to take account of couples as well as individual parents. Part II considers an approach to parenthood preparation which aimed to do just that.

PART TWO

An Approach to Parenthood Preparation

For groups, as well as for individuals, life itself means to separate and to be reunited, to change form and condition, to die and to be reborn. It is to act and to cease, to wait and rest, and then to begin acting again, but in a different way.

Arnold van Gennep

CHAPTER THREE

Preparing Couples for Parenthood

Even if there were an agreed body of knowledge about parenting to be transmitted (and there is not) and one could work on the assumption that knowledge always changes behaviour (which one cannot), it would still be necessary to bear in mind how much the inter-personal relationships and integrity of the parents affect their ability to be successful.

The Court Report

PREPARATION FOR PARENTHOOD

The Report of the Committee on Child Health Services, chaired by Professor Court, was one of a number of government publications during the 1970s (DHSS, 1974 and 1978; DES, 1977) which drew attention to a need for programmes of preparation for parenthood. The call for action gained momentum with a speech delivered in 1972 by the Secretary of State for Social Services, Keith Joseph, to the Pre-School Playgroup Association, in which he advocated intervention to break the *Cycle of Deprivation*, a term he used to describe the transmission of disadvantage from one generation to the next. This term was modified by Rutter and Madge (1976) to *Cycles of Disadvantage* in order the better to reflect the complex nature and aetiology of the phenomena it characterised.

The phrase *preparation for parenthood* is similar in its umbrella-like properties. It has been applied to a broad range of activities, ranging from those with an educational bias at one end of the spectrum, to those with a therapeutic emphasis at the other. (Pugh, 1980; Whitfield, 1980). Preparation for parenthood can encompass sex education for school children and marriage counselling for parents.

The Court Report, addressing itself to a narrower band of activities, commented upon the potential importance of classes for expectant parents, yet observed that, as currently organised, there was little objective evidence of any systematic construction of their content or, ultimately, of their value. While urging further study aimed at elucidating *what* parents need to know and *how* this information might best be transmitted, they urged that programmes of preparation for parenthood should be based on principles rather than prescriptions. To principles which have a bearing upon the *what* and *how* of intervention can be added those concerning *when* and *where* it might be expected to be effective.

The needs of parents are not easily determined and are likely to be idiosyncratic. Moreover, parents, in common with the rest of mankind, cannot be relied upon to behave rationally, and their use of resources will be affected by the social context in which services are offered. These factors indicate that the Court Report's emphasis on principle rather than prescription has relevance to any prospective programme of education for family life. This chapter will look at the considerations of principle which shaped one approach to preparation for parenthood. The discussion will look at the *what, how, when* and *where* of the approach, and will begin by considering its objective.

Intervention was planned with the intention of promoting the mental health of couples expecting their first baby. Some consideration of what is meant by mental health will provide a starting point for the discussion.

THE NATURE OF MENTAL HEALTH

Mental health has been depicted as a state of equilibrium between counterbalancing forces. A severe or chronic disturbance in this balance has been regarded as one indication of psychological illness. Winnicott (1971) emphasised that mental health is not a state of ease or absence of conflict, but is characterised by a capacity to experience fear as well as trust, pain as well as pleasure, doubt as well as certainty, and frustration as well as satisfaction. Parad and Caplan (1965) assert that 'at the appropriate time and place the presence of conflict and unhappiness is a criterion of mental health'. Similarly, Morris (1971) defines mental health as 'a developed capacity to deal with both internal conflict and external stress', resulting in an ability to 'love and work effectively', a phrase he attributes to Freud. The pursuit of mental health is neither a masochistic nor hedonistic activity, but one which is concerned with developing a tolerance of conflicting feelings and impulses, and with promoting a fuller awareness of, and capacity to become involved in, the various experiences of life.

Clinical and empirical studies have supported a view of mental health which incorporates a balance between positive and negative facets of experience. Janis (1958) showed that patients who were either morbidly anxious or, alternatively, unaffected by the prospect of surgery, recovered less well in the post-operative period than those who were moderately anxious and could worry creatively about the experience beforehand. Breen (1975) found that women who managed well in childbearing showed *more* feelings of insecurity and anxiety during pregnancy than those who experienced difficulties. She interpreted this finding as lending support to the view that awareness of anxiety and conflict before a transition enabled people to manage change well, and was a sign of psychological health. Her basic hypothesis was that the healthy woman is one who can modify her perception of herself, and her relationships with others, to take account of change.

In a community mental health context, Caplan's (1961) view of prevention similarly includes the notion of tolerance and avoids defining health in absolute terms. The objectives of reducing the risk of illness in the community (primary prevention), reducing the duration of established cases (secondary prevention), and minimising the effect of disablement (tertiary prevention) indicate gradations of therapeutic response to different and deteriorating levels of health.

Threats to mental health can come both from within and without, and in essence they constitute a prospect of imbalance. The psychoanalytic tradition has paid close attention to internal imbalance, and has addressed itself to aspects of repressed experience which can have a disturbing (but potentially creative) effect upon present-day life. Psychoanalytic therapy rests upon the assumption that controlled exposure to, and awareness of, these unconscious influences serve to reduce their grip over current feelings and behaviour, thereby creating greater freedom to participate in life.

Applied to marriage, psychoanalytic insights have provided a way of understanding interpersonal conflict in terms of the re-emergence, within a close relationship, of psychic preoccupations common to each partner. The capacity of one spouse to evoke and represent, in journalistic terms, 'the embodiment of the other's secret self, the living flesh upon the other's skeleton in the cupboard' (Tweedie, 1979), or, indeed, other figures from the past, has provided a basis for the claim that marriage affords particular opportunities for personal development (Woodhouse, 1975). There is an 'unconscious wisdom' (Sutherland, 1962) in marital choice which creates opportunities to anneal splits in the personality, to maintain in balance conflicting aspects of the self, and thereby to reduce the threat of repressed experience.

Other writers have turned their attention to external threats to mental health. Rapoport (1965) has drawn attention to the power of significant life events, like the birth of a baby, to induce a personal crisis. The word 'crisis' has been used in this context to denote what happens when an event overtaxes the capacity of an individual to cope. There follows a period of personal disorganisation in which old conflicts, symbolically linked with the present problem, are revived. With the opportunity to rework the past in relation to a current problem, it is possible to emerge from a crisis not only having mastered the exigencies of the present, but also having dealt more adequately than before with long-standing conflicts which may previously have been suppressed or repressed. Crises are therefore moments of opportunity as well as risk; they are not illnesses, although, as Rapoport (1965a) has observed, social convention sometimes leads us to define people in turmoil as ill.

When health is regarded as a state of balance, an analogy can be drawn between mental and physical states. In the field of medicine, an uncontaminated state of health would render a person extremely vulnerable to an environment populated by bacteria and viruses. To an extent, we rely upon infection for our protection. Without infection, there is no opportunity to generate a resistance which permits participation in life. Yet the notion of balance is crucial; there must be a capacity both to entertain and to withstand the infecting agent through the creation of antibodies, and this capacity will vary according to time and circumstance.

Immunology, as a branch of medicine, has made an important contribution to preventive health care. From a medical point of view the availability of different vaccines has made a full and extensive involvement with people and places less hazardous than it once was. Preventive intervention of this kind operates on the principle of exposing people to a modified virus of a disease in order to produce it in mild form and so stimulate the production of antibodies which will, in turn, afford future protection against that particular strain of infection.

In the field of mental health, exposure to avoided aspects of experience has been held to have similar properties. Extending the analogy with preventive medicine, the promotion of self-awareness, the encouragement of appropriate 'worry-work' and 'grief work' (Caplan, 1961) in relation to events, and the transmission of information relevant to critical periods of change, constitute a 'vaccine' for effective 'emotional inoculation' (Janis, 1958) against future mental ill-health. This analogy first derived from work undertaken in connection with people who had suffered an acute bereavement (Lindemann, 1944). Subsequently, it has been applied to programmes of ante-natal education and counselling, and it provided a model of intervention for the project team.

Some important questions follow from the analogy. Can intervention of this kind be harmful? Can the wish to eradicate illness unwittingly result in its creation? In the medical field a note of caution has been sounded. To a degree, tolerance of illness is socially determined. The 'onion' or 'iceberg' theory of sickness, referred to by Brearley (1978), suggests that even in the Western world our definition of illness covers only the visible outer layer or tip of an almost infinitely large whole. Accordingly, those described as healthy can be seen as simply not having been investigated enough. However, further investigations, delineations of illness or treatments carry the risk not only of adding to a growing category of iatrogenic illness, but of fostering an illness-oriented view of life (Kennedy, 1980). An extreme critic of medical intervention (Illich, 1975) comments that as people

> . . . require routine medical ministrations for the simple fact that they are unborn, newborn, infants, in their climacteric, or old, . . . life turns from a succession of different stages of health into a series of periods each requiring different therapies.

Can this criticism be applied to prospective schemes of intervention aimed at improving mental health?

The pattern of physical and mental illness in our society has placed a growing emphasis upon care, as opposed to cure (Brearley, 1978). Care implies human contact. Without human contact there can be no mental health. Prolonged periods of solitary confinement have a damaging effect upon the personality. Interaction with other people, what Caplan (1961) calls 'a social milieu', is a necessary condition of health. A sense of self is developed and maintained by a person's social relationships. To be where one is 'known' provides a degree of personal security and order which may not exist in alien surroundings. In so far as therapeutic services contribute towards defining a person's 'social milieu', the extent to which they have an elevating or depressing effect upon health will depend upon their nature rather than upon their presence or absence.

The case descriptions and research studies presented in the first part of this book suggest that the marital relationship has a special place in a person's 'social milieu'. By virtue of its intimate and durable nature, it has a capacity to facilitate the containment of internal conflict and external stress. One source of tension, consistently referred to by research studies concerned with the transition to parenthood, is the gap between the hopes and aspirations of expectant couples and their subsequent experience, a gap which can be greatest for those least equipped to reconcile themselves to the difference. In addressing themselves to this problem, perinatal services have tended to neglect the resource of the marital partnership, despite the *prima facie* case for encompassing couples, rather than just mothers, in their endeavours. Some attempts to enlarge the scope and content of services to include both husbands and wives have met with success. One study reported that husbands derived greater enjoyment from the prospect of parenthood in consequence (Russell, 1974), while others have claimed that classes have more impact when both men and women attend (Gordon *et al.*, 1960, 1965; Cyr and Wattenberg, 1965; Shereshefsky and Yarrow, 1973). Brown and Harris (1978) issued the challenge in these terms:

> While other factors such as marital difficulties and the quality of supportive ties would be more difficult to influence, they are in the longer term probably a better bet for some kind of intervention than most kinds of life events.

In taking up the challenge, the project team decided to address themselves to *couples* in an attempt to promote a healthy adaptation to parenthood. We planned to develop a programme which would not only support a central aspect of the social world of parents, their marriage, but which would also create a 'social milieu' to which they would be exposed.

The continuity afforded by marriage provides one reason why, as a social and psychological relationship, it can exercise a stabilising and maturing influence upon the individuals concerned. Continuity, as an organising principle, can therefore be applied to the provision of services. In a theoretical essay, Bain (1978) argues that the continuity and coherence of services available to people in transition do indeed have an important effect upon how change is managed. He uses the term 'social container' to describe both family and friends, and the network of formal services available to people at different periods of change in their lives. For expectant parents, the 'formal container' includes doctors, midwives, physiotherapists, dieticians, receptionists, health visitors and obstetricians. The way in which they interact together, and with the parents they serve, will determine the quality of an important aspect of the social container. Within this matrix, the project sought to find a place in which its aims might readily be integrated with the objectives of existing services, and which might afford some continuity between pre- and post-natal periods.

In so far as mental health describes a condition in which internal conflict and external stress are managed so that people may participate vigorously and effectively in life, it constituted the overall aim of the endeavour envisaged by the project team. To the extent that the 'social milieu' exerts an important influence upon health, *the project sought to enhance the capacity of marriage to contain the tensions and growing pains inherent in the process of adapting to change.* Within this general framework, specific issues concerning the *what, how, when* and *where* of one particular aspect of the project, the development of a group approach to couples expecting their first baby, will now be considered.

WHAT DO COUPLES NEED TO KNOW?

Information is a useful resource at any time, and particularly during periods of change when past certainties can no longer be relied upon so completely for the future. It can decrease a sense of helplessness and provide a guide to mastering new situations. For couples to know as much as possible about what parenthood entails makes good practical sense.

Some types of information are more unchanging and subject to generalisation than others. For example, the developments which take place in a woman's body during pregnancy can be described in a relatively straightforward way, as can the process of labour and delivery. Medical and dietary advice can be combined with information about where to go and what to expect of particular services. Up to a point it is possible to teach parentcraft skills: for example, how to feed a baby and change a nappy, and what to buy in preparation for the future. Direct information and advice of this sort can be invaluable to prospective parents and is already provided by hospitals and family health centres.

Yet even at this level complications arise. Information is usually conveyed within a relationship. A degree of power is vested in the teacher and there is an assumption of need in the recipient. How information is given and received within that relationship will affect, and be affected by, how the participants react to their ascribed roles. An assumption on the part of the teacher that she must always be 'in the know' may blind her to the resources of those she teaches. Different feelings about authority may prompt someone either to accept unquestioningly, or reject indiscriminately, advice proffered. Information is never a neutral commodity in social transactions. It will be credited or discredited according to its source, the manner in which it is given, and its particular meaning to the individual. Pines (1978) has warned of the dangers of soundly-based professional advice confusing new mothers if it does not correspond with their feelings towards their children. Richter (1976) comments upon the fallacy of approaching education as if parents were purely rational, duty-bound adults who need only to be better informed to succeed in their roles. On that basis, Morris (1971) is critical of the tendency in the educational system generally to split cognitive and affective aspects of learning, arguing that educationists and therapists have more in common than either care to admit.

If there are problems about communicating relatively straightforward information concerning tangible matters, they become much more acute when the information concerns personal feelings and family relationships. The likelihood that one person will accept the experience of another as relevant to him or herself is not high. Many of the research views assembled in the first part of this book, while conveying a considerable amount of information, stress that the nature of the experience of parenthood is subject to wide degrees of variation between individuals. The idiosyncratic nature of experience, and the complexity of factors which define the personal meaning ascribed to particular events, expose general statements about the effects of children upon family life to the criticism of being either simplistic or irrelevant.

Those who have attempted to tackle this problem have adopted different strategies. One study (Gordon *et al.*, 1960) designed a programme of systematic instruction for expectant mothers to prevent emotional difficulties after birth. The authors claimed considerable success for the scheme. A formal talk advised mothers to rest, to reduce their outside interests, to be less concerned with appearances and to avoid unnecessary chores or new responsibilities (like moving house or the care of dependent relatives). In addition, they were urged to register with a doctor and to use the links they had with family members, friends and young mothers. At the other extreme, Wilson (1968), in an exploratory study, set up groups in which his role as leader was confined to interpreting material which came from the mothers who attended. Behind these different approaches was a shared assumption that in times of change, people need what Marris (1974) has called a 'moratorium'. By this, he meant the time and space to take stock of a changed situation, to anticipate and monitor personal responses to change, and to explore new ways of meeting the challenge it brings.

In these circumstances, it is difficult to know whether it is the information, or the relationship within which that information is conveyed, which carries more weight. Gordon (1960) claimed that the programme established by himself and his colleagues owed its effectiveness to the advice and information the mothers received and not to the instructor or the setting. Similarly, Pringle (1980) asserts that preparation for parenthood is an activity which can be distinguished from support through a relationship. On the other hand, Chertok (1968) found from her study that interpersonal factors were at least as important as advice.

What is certain is that the way a relationship is established will itself communicate a message. Preparation classes organised in the day-time and directed towards mothers convey a clear message about the relevance of women, but relative unimportance of men, to this preparatory aspect of parenthood. In terms of what these classes offer at present, the implied message may be appropriate. It is in connection with the absence of classes relevant to needs of couples that a question is raised about such implicit communications, particularly when there is evidence to indicate that marriage can be an important influence upon parental adaptation.

Once the nature of the relationship between the preventive health services and parents is accepted as being an integral part of any communication which takes place between them, the issue can no longer be confined to what couples need to know about change (needs which, to some extent, they can be relied upon to formulate and articulate for themselves), but must include what practitioners consider to be the needs of those undergoing change. In this context, the project team identified four broad areas of psychological need during periods of change which influenced their subsequent work.

The first of these was that healthy adaptation requires an awareness of both the gains and losses, the good and bad feelings, which are precipitated by major events in a person's life. Major positive events, of which the birth of a child is a prime example for those who consciously want a baby, can be expected to precipitate ambivalent feelings and attitudes, and the tensions between these conflicting views and reactions need to be held in balance. It will be apparent from what has gone before that alongside the joy there exists an unacceptable face to parenthood which is often suppressed, and may only become visible when it reveals itself as identifiable breakdown. Freedom to acknowledge all aspects of experience, without self-recrimination or anxiety about alienation from others, is necessary to prevent suppression of what is feared to be unacceptable. Suppression carries the risk of fostering a malignant potential which may have disruptive effects in the future. Promoting a rounded awareness of the implications of change, in all its aspects, is likely to encourage a healthy adaptation.

Closely related is the need for appropriate 'worrying' and 'grieving', to use Caplan's words, so that those aspects of the past which are irreconcilable with, or inappropriate, to new circumstances can be relinquished, and those which provide a sense of continuity, purpose and meaning in life can be maintained. A process of this kind requires space to recognise and value those aspects which provide continuity, to mourn the loss of what is, for the time being at least, irrecoverable, and to be able to distinguish between the two. All change, however welcome, is likely to be facilitated by 'worrying' positively about future uncertainties and by 'grieving' for the lost past.

In the third place, it was assumed that change is less unsettling when experience conforms with expectation. Le Masters (1957) described parenthood as the real 'romantic complex' in our culture. Social images may reinforce individual discrepancies between fact and fantasy, although much has been done recently to counteract the idealisation of parenthood in society. Expectations about parenthood derive from conscious and unconscious aspects of family experiences in the past, as modified by information about parenthood, and contact with other parents, in the present. One way of modifying expectations is to bring together people undergoing the same process of change in their lives so that they may have access to information and experiences other than their own.

Finally, there is a need for some connection to be made between inner and outer resources. A person's inner resources are relatively constant and slow to change, developed as they are by the accumulation and interpretation of past experience. External resources are more malleable. There is, however, a relationship between the two which acts to promote or inhibit the use of both. People tend to strive actively to determine the nature and extent of their social environment so that it fits their personal assumptions about the world they inhabit; their social environment dictates the opportunities which are available to be taken up or turned down. Attempts to promote communication, within marriage and between expectant parents and the services available to them, need to take account of the inter-connectedness of inner and outer worlds if they are to enhance the future well-being of individuals and families.

These broad areas of need are easier to state than to translate into action. It would not be feasible, even if it were desirable, to chart a course which couples might follow in becoming parents, since the passage can be made in so many different ways. Nor is the problem just one of catering for a diversity of circumstances. The attitudes people have towards the future are born of emotional conviction stemming from experience. They reflect learned ways of coping with life which may or may not facilitate adaptation, but which define them as individuals. The issue is put by Sutherland (1971) in these terms:

> The 'self' is the term we use for that core of the personality that preserves continuity in change, and its integrity is what makes change acceptable. If this integrity of the self is threatened, change is resisted—often violently, as befits the defence of our most precious possession.

Programmes designed to promote family mental health are likely to be approached with caution because of the possibility that they will challenge cherished assumptions. The question of how to establish a link between couples and preventive health care services is therefore every bit as important as that which asks what they need to know.

On the basis of four assumptions about psychological need during periods of change, the project aimed to provide a 'moratorium' for couples in which there would be time for them to monitor their experience of pregnancy and early parenthood, either privately or through discussion, and so develop an awareness of change in the marital partnership which might in turn ease the transition from two to three.

HOW CAN LINKS BE ESTABLISHED?

Establishing links between couples and services involves forming relationships and encouraging effective communication within those relationships. The project sought to establish a link by setting up informal groups through which there might be a mutual exchange of information, while knowing that group approaches have their limitations.

What is known about existing ante-natal classes for groups of mothers suggests that it is the older, better-educated middle-class women who respond (Russell, 1974; Brimblecombe, 1975; Cartwright, 1975; Richter, 1976; Pugh, 1980). A situation therefore exists in which those identified by research studies as most vulnerable to transitional stress (young mothers and those from social class IV and V) are least likely to avail themselves of professional help. In her review of current initiatives in the field of preparation for parenthood, Pugh (1980) refers to studies which suggest that the take-up rate of ante-natal classes as a whole may be in the region of only 40 per cent of those eligible to attend.

Brimblecombe (1975) noted in a different context the inverse relationship between the availability and take-up of health care services and the extent of need, resourceful families being better equipped than their needier counterparts to know what help was available and from where it was to be obtained. Compounding this problem was a tendency for affluent areas to be better served than poor areas by professional resources. Yet Stacpoole (in Pugh 1980) repudiated any notion that the ill-balanced take-up of services could be explained solely in terms of one social group hogging resources at the expense of another. He proposed that those who needed but failed to make use of services in the community were intrinsically difficult to reach.

The difficulty in reaching those in need of help has been explained in both social and psychological terms. Cartwright (1975) suggests that working-class families find the preventive health services irrelevant to their needs, and alienating; she asserts that they are much more likely to turn towards relatives or friends for help. Brearley (1978) supports this view, while acceding that they are often not well informed about available services in their area. He goes on to suggest that middle-class families are more likely to plan ahead, to save, and generally to be orientated towards the future than working-class families. This future orientation makes them more likely to use preventive services than those who have a present-day orientation to life, and who tend to regard what happens to them as the consequence of fate or some other design outside their control. Richter (1976) expresses a similar view, as does Rainwater (1960) in connection with class attitudes towards contraception.

The extent of control which a person experiences over his or her life has psychological as well as social roots. If a sense of personal autonomy is fragile, the prospect of outside intervention may be threatening. Russell (1974) found that those who did not reply to her research questionnaire were usually young, pre-maritally pregnant and under stress. Frommer and O'Shea (1973b) established that an experience of childhood separation increased a woman's vulnerability to stress and reduced the likelihood that she would receive effective help from the statutory services. This reluctance to use available services was explained by the observation that, as a group, these women were less aware of their needs and anxieties than others who adapted more easily.

Similarly Breen's (1975) study of first-time mothers found that those most at risk were also least likely to change their perceptions of themselves and others and were least likely to admit their own imperfections and anxieties. In addition they were most likely to polarise parental images into extremes which approximated the fairy godmothers and witches of childhood.

Paradoxically, a poor experience of being parented, and a consequent desire to do better for one's own children, can result in the setting of unrealistically high parental standards by those least equipped to match them. Subsequent failure to live up to an ideal may result in a self-imposed isolation to conceal failure both from oneself and from others. The problem may be compounded by a social climate which promotes a rosy picture of parenthood and values self-sufficiency.

It would, of course, be misleading to evaluate response to an invitation to participate in any relationship purely on the basis of a sociological or psychological typecasting of the client group. Response is importantly affected by perceptions of the service being offered. Wilson (1968) refers to a survey of maternity services in Great Britain in which clinic attendance was considered to be more a function of the clinic than the mothers attending. Even if parents can be persuaded to attend (and France, for example, has succeeded in attracting parents to pre- and post-natal clinics by offering financial payment), attendance alone is no guarantee of useful classes.

It makes sense to assume that people will more readily engage with others in considering the personal implications of change when they can be sure that their position will be accepted and understood. Parkes (1971) has observed that those undergoing change are most likely to be helped by others who have had first-hand experience of the particular transition they are facing. Caplan (1978) has suggested that the professional might take more of a back seat in providing support services, and develop his role as a catalyst, bringing together people who can help each other. Herself a mother, Oakley (1979b) discovered that her research interest in other mothers had the effect of changing their experience of perinatal care. The development of self-help groups of many different kinds (see Hiskins, 1980), and particularly the National Childbirth Trust in connection with parenthood, lends weight to the view that links are most easily established between those in like circumstances.

Then, again, some people will prefer to do their own homework privately, and some not at all. Russell (1974) and Cartwright (1975), for example, were surprised at the extent to which parents drew upon books for information. The development of media education, such as the recent Open University courses for parents with children of different ages, has increased the scope for drawing privately upon information resources.

Despite the constraints upon individuals in groups, the project team considered there was still a strong case for offering a public forum for discussion. Having decided that, they had to decide how structured the meetings would be. There is evidence that structured programmes of intervention are more appreciated and effective than geared exclusively towards offering support or promoting insight. Shereshefsky and Yarrow (1973) found that attempting to evoke an experience in advance, by outlining likely reactions to birth and parenthood, was a more successful aid to adaptation than was interpretation aimed at promoting insight, or clarification of feelings and problems. Gordon and his colleagues (1959) arrived at similar conclusions from their study of the individual treatment of emotional disturbance during pregnancy.

As we have seen, they also found that systematic instruction of ordinary expectant mothers had a positive and long-lasting influence upon their post-partum emotional adaptation (Gordon et al., 1960, 1965). Good outcome was associated with attendance at these instruction periods: only 15 per cent of those who attended experienced post partum emotional upsets, as compared with 37 per cent of the control group.

At the other end of the spectrum, Wilson (1968) adopted an interpretative role in relation to his group of mothers, many of whom he saw weekly for more than a year. His aim was to develop conditions of sufficient security (what he called 'stable privacy') to allow mothers to tolerate uncertainty and draw upon their own experiences rather than those of others. The emphasis was not upon instruction, but upon preserving space, and in that sense imposing a structure within which the creativity of the group members was given an opportunity to develop. From his experience he asked:

> Is it too simple an observation to make that confident expectations of continuity in a defined acceptable relationship is one of the main psychological conditions of privacy, and necessary for relaxation of what is sometimes described as the silent inaccessibility of the pregnant woman?

These two experiences posed a dilemma for the project team. As psycho-analytically orientated marital therapists, their working philosophy accorded more closely with Wilson's model than with that of the Gordons. However, Wilson's model presupposed a very heavy commitment in terms of time, resources and skill which was incompatible both with the limited intervention which the project envisaged, and the intention that the model, if successful, might be applied elsewhere within the scope of existing services.

The problem was resolved by attempting to combine the best of both worlds. *The project team proposed offering a limited number of group meetings to couples expecting their first baby, the number being compatible with the resources of existing services to continue the meetings if they proved useful once the project came to an end. In these groups, the project team envisaged a combination of educational and interpretative skills through a working partnership between a health visitor or visitors and one or two members of the project team. This partnership would lead the groups, but in a way which attempted to respond to the preoccupations of the members rather than to institute a formal programme of instruction. The project team would not restrict their contribution to interpretation, but would actively promote and support discussion in the groups.* Active leadership of this sort is in keeping with what is known about the specific needs of groups for married couples (Cochrane, 1973; Skynner, 1973). The compromise resembled Caplan's (1951) work with mothers, in which he attempted both to convey information and to put questions back to his groups, so that members might draw upon their own resources.

WHEN IS INTERVENTION LIKELY TO BE EFFECTIVE?

The maternity services have developed in a way which pays maximum attention to the last trimester of pregnancy and to the period of confinement. The careful monitoring of mother and baby during pregnancy allows for the detection and prevention of conditions which might otherwise make birth a hazardous passage.

Ante-natal education programmes and psychoprophylactic exercises encourage mothers to participate in labour in a way which eases delivery. Analgesics are available to control pain and even to provide a sense-free experience of childbirth. The science and technology of medicine is at hand when a baby is born. In microcosm, the arrival of a baby in the delivery room signifies the fundamental change which occurs when two become three. It is an observable, sharply-focussed event which is normally completed in hours following a relatively short period of gestation. A concentrated medical response can ensure that birth is a safe, and, with luck, satisfying experience. A biological process determines when services will be made available.

In contrast, the passage a couple has to make in successfully managing the social and psychological implications of becoming a family of three is neither a tangible nor a readily observable process. It can take years instead of hours to complete, and is affected by an antecedent history as long as the life-times of the parents. While a poor 'birth passage' for the family can result in future damage and handicap, there are few social or psychological guides to the timing of intervention which carry the same imperative as a biological process.

Psychoprophylactic classes for childbirth rest on the assumption that knowledge about the stages of labour and the process of delivery, and involvement in rehearsal exercises, act to increase control over an unfamiliar event, to diminish fear of the unknown and to provide a release from elements of fantasy which invariably surround childbirth. Less fear means less tension, which, in turn, is likely to mean an easier delivery. Intervention necessarily precedes birth because its objective is to facilitate the baby's arrival.

Drawing an analogy with psychoprophylaxis, the project team proposed that by encouraging couples to reflect upon the changes affecting their lives, to articulate their half-formulated anxieties, and to know more about their ambivalent feelings, the birth passage of the new family unit would be eased. The analogy suggested that birth would be the pivotal event and intervention should precede it. Since it was intended to integrate intervention of this kind with existing ante-natal classes, the last three months of pregnancy were the operative period.

However, two other factors were taken into consideration. In the first place, and for reasons already given, continuity was regarded as an essential require-ment of service provision. Some contact with couples after their baby was born was therefore important if they were to be seen through a process of change. In the second place, it is known that people are more amenable to outside inter-vention and social learning at some times than they are at others (Rapoport *et al.*, 1977). Some match between what services offer and the developmental preoccupations of individuals is likely to result in the best outcome. Caplan has suggested that a limited intervention can be particularly effective and acceptable during critical periods of change when people may be temporarily disorganised and engaged in working out new ways of managing in altered circumstances (1961, 1964). He originally proposed that crises of the type to which he was referring lasted no more than six weeks, but regarded pregnancy and birth as a relevant process since pregnancy was a period of increased susceptibility to crisis. The crisis of parenthood was regarded as a blanket term, covering a cluster of associated crises such as leaving work, giving birth, and assuming responsibility for the life of a helpless infant. Some of these subsidiary crises would occur before the event of birth, some after. Since aspects of parenthood are 'developmental crises', as opposed to sudden, unexpected 'accidental crises' (Erikson, 1959), Caplan and other crisis theorists argue that intervention should precede as well as follow the event in order to encourage realistic anticipation of changes which might be expected to follow.

On the basis of an analogy drawn with psychoprophylactic classes for childbirth, and in the light of crisis theory, the project team decided that birth would be regarded as the pivotal event for change in the marriage, and that intervention on a group basis would be timed to span the last three months of pregnancy and no more than the first six months of the baby's life. This period coincided with one in which health care services available to expectant parents were more active, and in consequence provided the best chance of integrating the groups with existing programmes of perinatal care.

WHERE SHOULD GROUPS BE BASED?

Nearly all first-time mothers have their babies in hospital. They are the women most likely to make use of ante-natal services, very probably at the hospital where their confinement is planned. Most hospitals with a maternity unit would have provided a sufficient number of first-time parents for the proposed groups. They therefore suggested themselves as a suitable base.

However, continuity of care in a large hospital was by no means guaranteed. Anecdotal accounts of busy ante-natal clinics, long waits for brief examinations, and contradictory advice received from ever-changing staff were sufficiently frequent to question whether, from either the parents' or project's point of view, hospitals would provide an amenable environment for the work envisaged. Moreover, hospitals were large, complex, and, to many people, intimidating institutions, which trade in illness and disability, not in health and life. Additional to these environmental problems were practical problems resulting from the fact that once a mother returns home from hospital, she is unlikely to have any further contact with the maternity department where her baby was born apart from a routine check-up between one and two months after birth. Even if it was appropriate and desirable for hospitals to be active in the post-natal period, for those parents who lived a long way away there would be considerable practical difficulties in maintaining the link.

Following discharge from hospital, it is the midwives, the health visitors and the family doctors who take over. The break in service provision coincides almost precisely with the period of maximum change for the mother and the family unit. Poor communication between hospital and community services can sometimes emphasise the disruption. The community services may themselves perpetuate a fragmented experience of care if their rate of staff turnover is high. Recognition of the problem of discontinuity has prompted some areas to develop 'shared care' schemes in which a family doctor may monitor his patient's pregnancy until shortly before her confinement, and may even go with her to the hospital to deliver her baby. As a community-based practitioner, the family doctor is, perhaps, in the best position to provide continuous medical care for the family. His or her role is supplemented by that of the health visitor, whose function encompasses social and psychological aspects of family health. Health visiting services are comprehensive, and not restricted to families with identified problems. This gives them an important preventive function in the community.

While an affiliation with community-based family health services offered the best hope of continuity, it was not easy for the project team to find health centres in London where ante-natal classes were flourishing. Several centres reported that the drift towards hospital confinement, the development of National Childbirth Trust classes, or the lack of interest of the indigenous population had led to their demise. They had 'died a natural death', in the words of one health visitor. In one centre where classes were still held, they ran in conjunction with a doctor's ante-natal clinic, and the health visitor responsible for them betrayed her discouragement when she said that they had the status of a 'waiting room activity'. Yet she believed that ante-natal contact with families was 'worth its weight in gold', although the means for effecting this was not always clear.

In Caplan's (1961, 1964) terms, the position of health visitors in the primary health care team makes them 'key mental health workers'. Working in family health centres, which are located in the neighbourhood of those they serve, health visitors are accessible to parents during pregnancy and the early months of parenthood. *Guided by the principle of continuity and the need to collaborate and integrate the groups with existing activities of key workers, the project team decided to base the groups for couples in family health centres.* Centres were selected where, contrary to current trends, ante-natal classes were reasonably active.

AN APPROACH TO PREPARING COUPLES FOR PARENTHOOD

In the light of the previous discussion, the project team decided to approach a group of health visitors to ask their reactions to the proposal that they share in the development of a preventive model of intervention geared to the needs of couples expecting their first baby. To this end, the Council for the Education and Training of Health Visitors was contacted for its views upon the relevance of the proposed discussion groups to the work of health visitors, and for its reactions to the development of a collaborative working link between a marital agency and a community nursing agency. The Council showed interest in the proposal and contacted several Area Nursing Officers in London to see how they would react. An interested response from four areas led to discussions with each and finally a decision was taken to carry out the work in one of these areas.

Nine months after discussions began with staff in that area, workshops were set up for health visitors and the project team. They provided a forum for considering some of the opportunities, constraints and dilemmas affecting health visitors in their day to day work with families. In so far as the project team drew attention to the implications of marriage for the work of health visitors, their function resembled Caplan's (1964) 'mental health consultations'. The workshops are discussed in Chapter Five.

In addition, a series of discussion programmes were offered by health visitors and the project team to couples during late pregnancy and the early months of parenthood. They were run from four community-based family health centres along lines which have been indicated. The group approach to preparing couples for parenthood will be considered in Chapter Four.

From the discussion group themes it was intended to compile a booklet which might help couples who were unlikely to attend the groups but who might do their homework privately. In the event, these groups did not provide adequate material, and so a questionnaire was designed and circulated to couples served by the four centres at which the groups were held. The aim of the questionnaire was to assemble first-hand accounts of the ways in which the arrival of a baby changed the lives and marital partnerships of couples. Material drawn from the replies formed the prologue to this book.

CHAPTER FOUR

A Group Approach

First mother: I would like to have been given more help about having *had* a baby. The baby was the magic goal and preparation was up to the birth. I was not prepared for my feelings afterwards apart from post-natal depression! This nebulous term covered everything, it seemed.

There was no preparation regarding returning to a normal married life after nine months of something other than; when to resume sexual intercourse, how you would feel, etc. All preparation heralded the coming of the baby but when it came I found that I was asking questions that should have been answered before the baby's arrival. I was certainly unprepared for the adjustment that I would have to make.

Second mother: It's something that you can't learn about or find out about until you have your own child. People can talk to you about what to do and how you'll feel . . . and it's all wasted, because it doesn't relate to your experience. I went to ante-natal classes . . . and the teacher there talked to us a little about the impact of the baby, and I remember not even listening; I couldn't even bring myself to listen properly because I thought this won't happen to me . . . it didn't relate at all.

Both these mothers attended preparation classes while they were expecting their first child, yet neither felt that they had been sufficiently prepared for the impact of a baby upon their lives. One attributed this lack of preparedness to deficiencies in the scope of the classes she attended, implying that the problem could be overcome by a more comprehensive coverage of the issues involved. The other believed that it was impossible to anticipate the experience.

The attempt to broaden the scope of existing ante-natal classes, described in this chapter, throws some light upon the dilemma represented by these divergent views. The conclusion drawn is that preparation for the emotional effects of parenthood means helping to establish a network of relationships for couples which can be drawn upon when the need arises. As an educative strategy, its usefulness may be more limited than is sometimes supposed.

The programmes will be discussed with reference to how they were presented, the response they elicited, the use to which they were put and the evaluation made by those who participated. A brief description of the offer made to couples, and the centres where the programmes were held, serves to set the scene.

THE OFFER

A series of discussion meetings were offered to couples expecting their first baby. The meetings were held in the evening at four community health centres in West London and were affiliated with classes already running there. A complete programme consisted of at least six one and a half hour meetings, which spanned late pregnancy and the early months of parenthood. They were led by a partnership between the health visitors and the project team.

THE SETTINGS

The four health centres were situated within a few miles' radius of each other in a heavily populated area of outer London. They were selected on the basis that they served a reasonably stable and ethnically balanced population, and were capable of providing access to sufficient couples to make the enterprise viable. It was also important that they already offered ante-natal classes.

The original intention was to hold groups at two large centres. The first of these was Mattock Lane health centre which housed six health visitors, one of whom worked on a part-time basis. The area it served was predominantly middle-class, and as a centre it was considered by the health visitors to offer a high degree of job satisfaction. 'If you can't get a group of parents together at Mattock Lane, you won't anywhere else,' remarked one health visitor with a tinge of envy. Her impression was that parents attended classes there in droves, and that they had a receptive attitude towards ante-natal care. While the staff at Mattock Lane hesitated to make quite the same judgement, they anticipated that there would be little difficulty in providing sufficient couples for three or four programmes during the eighteen-month period in which the project was to run.

It was during an early planning meeting between the Mattock Lane staff and the two (women) members of the project team who proposed working there that a health visitor from the neighbouring Laurel House clinic expressed interest in running a group. Although Laurel House was a smaller clinic (housing two full-time and one part-time health visitors) and had access to relatively few prospective parents, it was agreed to make the attempt there as well. One member of the project team attached herself to the Mattock Lane centre and the other to Laurel House clinic.

The remaining two project workers (a man and a woman) approached Hanwell health centre in the hope of setting up groups there. Hanwell was a modern, purpose-built health centre, housing doctors, nurses, midwives, dental staff, and receptionists, as well as seven full-time and three part-time health visitors.

It was situated in a heavily-built up area and, in contrast with the predominantly middle-class population served by Mattock Lane and Laurel House, catered for a district in which there was considerable social and ethnic diversity. The health centre had been burgled on occasions, and because of security considerations, one of the chronic difficulties in running evening groups was keeping the doors unlocked so that couples could get in.

At the first planning meeting, the project workers had a remarkably similar experience to their colleagues at Mattock Lane and Laurel House. A health visitor from the neighbouring but smaller Islip Manor clinic proposed that groups should be run there as well as at Hanwell. Islip Manor clinic was housed in a large attractive old building and had a staff of three health visitors assisted by a midwife and a woman doctor who visited the clinic on a sessional basis. Again it was decided to include the smaller centre in the project, despite the relatively few couples upon whom the groups might hope to draw for support.

In contrast to their colleagues, the two workers attached to Hanwell and Islip Manor maintained their partnership and ran groups together at both centres. Initially they did not include a health visitor in the running of the groups because they were interested to learn whether a male/female partnership would affect the outcome, and they did not want to over-weight the leadership. They quickly realised their mistake, however, and subsequent programmes were led jointly by them and at least one health visitor. The importance of an integrated partnership between health visitors and the project team will be referred to later.

HOW THE PROGRAMMES WERE PRESENTED

There were three principal ways in which the purpose of the discussion groups was conveyed to couples: the first was by means of letter or printed invitation; the second was through existing ante-natal groups for parents; the third was by individual personal contact between a health visitor and (usually) a mother. While no centre relied exclusively upon any one of these methods, there were marked differences in the approach predominantly used by each. Generally speaking, women were between five and eight months pregnant at the time they and their husbands were invited to attend the discussion groups.

The Mattock Lane centre relied heavily upon a written communication to invite eligible couples to the groups. A stencilled invitation was circulated which read as follows:

ARE YOU EXPECTING YOUR FIRST BABY?
An open invitation to expectant parents to attend a series of discussion meetings on starting a family. The aims of the meetings are threefold:

1. To meet other couples living locally who are expecting their first baby around the same time.
2 For couples to reflect upon and share with each other the changes experienced in moving from being two to becoming a family of three.
3 To anticipate the rewards and satisfactions of starting a family and also the accompanying strains that affect most families. Anticipation of both helps keep the whole event in perspective!
The programme will consist of six meetings, three to be held during pregnancy and three after your baby is born. The meetings will be informal and will be held at the Mattock Lane health centre.

There followed dates for the early meetings and a tear-off slip to return to the centre. In contrast, the smaller Laurel House clinic issued no written invitation and relied solely on personal contact between health visitor and mother or couple to pass on information about the groups and to invite attendance.

At Hanwell, different approaches were tried but, as at Mattock Lane, a written invitation was used most frequently. Although worded differently, a stencilled invitation saying much the same as that used by the Mattock Lane centre was issued for the early programmes. It was distributed either by post or by health visitors, some of whom had no direct contact with the project team and therefore could not be expected to supplement the printed invitation except by their second-hand impressions of what was intended.

At Islip Manor, invitations were issued directly to couples, usually through groups which had been convened with the purpose of showing a film or slides about childbirth. At the end of the evening, an invitation to the discussion groups would be issued by the project workers in conjunction with those health visitors who were present. The advantage of this method was that the parents were able to take stock of each other and the leaders, and could ask questions to clarify aspects of the programme about which they were not clear. The leaders often shared with couples the newness of the venture, and their hope that what was learned from the meetings might help other couples in their position.

It will be clear that in presenting the discussion groups to couples, the project team relied heavily upon health visitors and their understanding of the purpose of the meetings. In the early stage of the project both they and the project team were working out what sort of a partnership they might have and mistakes were sometimes made.

One such mistake was the decision, referred to earlier, to exclude health visitors from the leadership of the early groups held at the Hanwell and Islip Manor centres. At a meeting convened to discuss this error, one of the health visitors described how difficult it had been to invite people to groups in which she was not participating and about which she knew very little. She and her colleagues had preconceptions about the groups existing for parents with problems. They wondered how invasive the leaders might be. A note left outside one of the clinics, directing couples to the 'Marital Studies Group', demonstrated how separate from the normal activities of the centre the meetings were seen as being, and how easily their purpose could be misconstrued. The lack of integration of the early meetings affected the extent to which health visitors recommended the groups to families they knew, and in consequence affected the rate of response at that early stage.

RESPONSE

During the twenty-one-month life of the project, fifteen attempts were made to launch programmes, of which six completed their full term of meetings. The response to each programme is detailed in Appendix III, Table I. The figures suggest that relatively few of the pregnant population in the areas concerned came in contact with the groups. For example, at Islip Manor there were 98 notifications of primiparous live births in a fifteen-month period commencing three months after the project started. In all, 62 invitations were known to have been issued, 38 for the two programmes which ran full term. From these, 13 couples and 2 women attended one or more meetings of these two completed programmes. While the most generous rate of response to these two programmes can be estimated at 39 per cent (on the basis of those invited and those who attended at least once), the overall figures give an indication of the small scale of the enterprise. Subsequent discussion therefore needs to be qualified by the limited nature of the experience.

The ages and social class characteristics of those who attended the six complete programmes appear in Appendix III, Table II. On the whole, the women were well above the average age for bearing a first child (which is 25 in the United Kingdom), they tended to be well-educated, and nearly all had given up work, often of a professional nature, to start a family. In terms of age and social class they were similar to those noted by other studies as the most frequent users of ante-natal services. This was only to be expected for those groups which were recruited directly from existing day-time classes for mothers.

One of the significant differences between the programmes and reports of other ante-natal classes is their degree of success in attracting men to the meetings, particularly during pregnancy. It was unusual for a man not to accompany his wife to at least one of the meetings, and most came as frequently as their wives. This indicates that services directed towards couples, as opposed just to mothers, are capable of encouraging a joint response, and that men may not be as intrinsically inaccessible as is sometimes supposed.

However, families from lower socio-economic groups, those whom research findings suggest are particularly vulnerable to stress, were conspicuous by their absence. In terms of social class characteristics, those parents who attended might have been expected to have the resources to seek out available services as well as the inclination to use them. At one level it is therefore reasonable to conclude that the programmes attracted couples who least needed to come. Yet that would be to foreclose on some important issues raised by the experience.

Our interest was not primarily in sociological factors affecting response, but in the psychological factors which had a bearing both upon response and upon how the groups were used. Attending discussion groups may well be a more familiar pastime to mortgagees than council tenants, but the purpose of the groups was to draw attention to changes affecting marriage, and this might be perceived as highlighting aspects of becoming a parent which cause anxiety. The possibility that the response to and use of the groups reflects wider issues relevant to the management of change will be considered later.

Response not only indicated the degree of interest in the offer, but also reflected upon the way invitations were made. Of the four centres which ran programmes it was the two smaller ones (which were nearly overlooked because they were not considered capable of providing access to sufficient couples) which were responsible for four of the six completed series of meetings. As a general observation, health visitors at the smaller centres were able to contact couples on a personal basis more frequently than their colleagues at the larger centres, since the number of those to be contacted was smaller. Moreover, at the small centres it was possible for all the staff to feel involved with and actively to participate in the project. In contrast, only a minority of staff at the large centres shared in the running of groups, which meant that the pro- grammes were less securely held, less clearly understood and invited less interest than in the small centres. Sometimes the size of the centre would affect com- munication between colleagues. For example, when the last programme was launched at Hanwell, it was discovered that another health visitor, temporarily attached to the centre, had established a class of her own from amongst those who were to be invited to the programme meetings.

Other factors also had a bearing upon response. It seemed that large groups demanded less of members and tolerated absences better than small groups, and were therefore more likely to complete their full term of meetings. Some- times an informal leader appeared within a group and kept the members in touch between meetings, maintaining a sense of group identity. Once or twice the impetus was lost because of a long gap between meetings occasioned by summer holidays.

Different approaches had their drawbacks: one meeting convened at Islip Manor for the purpose of issuing invitations was dominated by a couple who were expecting a second child and had had a poor experience of hospital treat- ment when their previous child was born. They were generally sceptical about the ability of classes to be of much help and this had a discouraging effect upon those present who might otherwise have been prepared to try the groups for

themselves. Once the competing claims on evenings and the effects of illness or
bad weather are added to these factors, the impossibility of selecting any one
explanation for the low rate of response becomes apparent. To have expected
the groups to appeal to all sections of the expectant community would, in any
case, have been highly unrealistic.

Common to all the completed programmes was a marked decline in attendance at the post-natal meetings. Again one might point for explanation
towards the greater practical difficulties of getting out with a young baby, the
increased value of time to oneself in the evenings and the prevailing state of
exhaustion common in the early months of parenthood. Yet the way the
meetings were used during pregnancy and after suggests that changes were
taking place which themselves had a bearing upon receptiveness and response.

HOW THE GROUPS WERE USED

The ante natal meetings

The ante-natal meetings were characterised by a *togetherness* between couples
and a reluctance, often shared by the leaders, to pursue subjects which were
potentially disturbing.

The sense of togetherness in the groups had three aspects. The first of these
was indicated by a relatively high degree of homogeneity, in terms of age and
social class characteristics, amongst those who attended the groups which persisted longest (see Appendix III, Table II). This homogeneity was normally
matched by a high degree of consensus between the views expressed by couples
at the meetings.

When there were sharp differences of opinion, there was a tendency for those
who did not feel 'at one' with the group to withdraw. The groups run at the
Laurel House centre illustrate the point. The ten couples who attended the two
series of discussion groups held there might all be described as solidly middle-
class. Despite occasional absences from meetings, only one couple withdrew
completely. The wife, Mrs Sand, had conveyed her reservations about the
groups from the outset. When the health visitor had invited her to the
meetings, the reply she had received was that the couple would give them a try
but she thought the groups sounded much too middle-class for her. At the first
meeting Mrs Sand became embroiled in a discussion, which later began to
assume the proportions of an argument, about whether or not mothers should
return to work. She asserted that she wished to return to work as soon as
possible after her baby was born. Perhaps because she was a lone voice representing her particular view, she became 'spikier' as the evening went on and
critical of the lack of (State) help for mothers with young babies who wanted to
work full-time. Despite the efforts of the leaders, the two points of view

became polarised. Her husband, who had accompanied her to the meetings, did not participate in the discussion and remained quiet throughout. Neither partner attended subsequent meetings.

Not only was there pressure to be together as a group, but also there was pressure to be together as a couple in the meetings. There was little expression of differences between a husband and wife about, for example, their attitudes towards future support from their parents, or in the way they imagined their life together once the baby was born. Explicit reference to change or tensions in marriage was rare. Often, partners would draw their chairs close to each other at the meetings and there would be some physical contact between them. It was more likely that both husband and wife would attend the ante-natal meetings than the post-natal meetings. Frequently, one partner would speak on behalf of the pair. Generally speaking, the men were more active than the women in discussions.

Sometimes it seemed as if the *idea* of a baby provided a common preoccupation which served to draw couples and partners together in the way they considered their future life and relationships. At other times, an *idea* of themselves as parents could serve a similar purpose. In the following example, recorded very shortly before their baby was born, one of the few references in the groups to the disturbance of an *idea* of parenthood was made by a husband who saw his marriage changing in a disconcertingly predictable way:

> Mr Frank was worried about his wife's determination not to return to work for a year, thinking that she might vegetate, He reminded her of their shared response to couples who only seemed able to talk 'baby talk' and their vow never to be like that. He also thought that at the end of one year she might want another year off work.*

This example was an exception to the general rule of 'sticking together' in the groups. Usually, the hope invested in the idea of parenthood served as a unifying bond between those who had yet to experience the reality of life with a young baby.

Finally, there were more general indications of a wish for togetherness in marriage, suggesting that for some it was a feature of married life during pregnancy outside the groups. The following is a case in point:

> At first Mrs Seaton had hated the whole business of pregnancy. She had been violently sick daily for weeks, and could not believe what was happening to her. Mr Seaton said quietly: 'I felt so left out.'
> The rest of the group expostulated that he surely could not have wanted to be involved in the sickness. He said that he had; it would have been better than feeling so excluded and he thought he would probably have managed it better than his wife. She agreed. She had felt so ill and there seemed no reason for it. She was asked

---

* These, and subsequent insertions, are taken from notes made by the project team after each meeting had ended.

whether she had been looking for sympathy. Mrs Seaton replied: 'I felt awful, but I did play on it too. I know I did. It seemed so *unfair* to feel so bad when you couldn't show anything to prove you were justified.'

Taken in all three aspects, the togetherness of couples as it appeared in a group context during pregnancy made the task of reflecting upon change within marriage a difficult one to pursue. The need to be together was incompatible with a focus which might reveal difference. The capacity of pregnancy and the prospect of birth to draw couples together has been commented upon by research studies reviewed earlier.

The other, and related, main feature of the ante-natal groups was a reluctance to discuss subjects which might raise anxiety. A wish to create a safe environment was reflected not only in the relative absence of differences expressed by couples, but also in the way birth and the newborn baby were handled in anticipation. For example, this attempt to encourage talk about birth and its immediate aftermath resulted in a discussion which jumped ahead of its subject:

> It was very hard to keep concentrating on the impending births, and the general drift of the discussion veered more and more to the difficulties which were likely to be encountered when babies had become too big for carrycots, or were toddlers, or had started school, or were showing the problems of teenagers! We tried to go along with their preoccupations and describe how anxieties varied at different stages of development, but we also commented that they had leapt over the next few weeks/months into a more comfortable distant future, and perhaps this was a good way of avoiding more imminent worries. They seemed ready to accept this, but could not do anything to focus themselves on present anxieties, and we did not push it further.

Sometimes it was difficult to know whether this tendency to jump ahead indicated anxiety about birth, and therefore a wish to avoid the subject, or an effort on the part of those present to prepare themselves by recovering aspects of their remembered childhood experience. At other times it was less difficult. For example, reference was made to the danger of 'counting your chickens before they're hatched', or of tempting providence by assuming a live birth and healthy baby:

> One husband asked if anyone had seen a television programme about a woman who had spent £200 on things for a baby she was going to adopt and the adoption had fallen through. There was a lot of feeling about this . . . all seemed to have some idea of the names they might choose for their babies but not one ventured to put it into words.

This response suggested an intrinsic reluctance to anticipate positive aspects of parenthood for fear of presuming upon good fortune.

Similarly, negative experiences, such as anxiety about the possibility of damage or pain during childbirth, tended to be referred to only in the post-natal meetings when the survival and health of mother and baby were assured.

Nor was it just the women who indicated these fears. During one of the meetings at which invitations to a series of group discussions were combined with the showing of a film on childbirth, one of the men present kept his eyes shut during the delivery scenes. In the discussion which followed he challenged a health visitor about the amount of pain experienced during labour and birth, suggesting that too much was made of it and that the process could be relatively painless. He subsequently attended discussion meetings with his wife and made it clear that he would not be present when their baby was born since that was the 'woman's job'. However, the reference he made to birth as a 'bull fight' and the mention that his mother had nearly died giving birth to him suggested that he was more anxious about birth than he cared to admit.

There is an anomaly in the situation where a man wants to leave childbirth entirely to his wife yet attends a film and discussion with her about that very issue. This and other instances suggested to the project team that many couples were ambivalent towards the possibility of learning more about their hopes for and fears of the future. Occasionally, given a small group and an atmosphere of confidence, an important experience would be shared. One example of this was at the Islip Manor centre where, after an evening discussion had started in a light-hearted way, one of two husbands present queried whether they were the people who really needed the groups. He asked if the leaders' assessment of some of the potential hazards of parenthood had been overstated for most ordinary couples. The leaders stuck to what they had said before, and the discussion then took a serious turn in which both men said that at different times they had felt depressed during their wives' pregnancies. They went on to talk about the absence of fathers for themselves, or grandfathers for their expected children, because of death or divorce. The prospect of fatherhood re-surrected for these men their loss of some aspects of the experience of being fathered, upon which they might otherwise have drawn when they became fathers themselves.

More often, the group leaders picked up a sense that couples did not wish to be disturbed, and on occasions felt constrained from speaking as they might otherwise have done. When they did speak about what they thought the group would not want to hear, they were likely to be told they were taking an exaggeratedly depressing stance, or, alternatively, to be greeted by a lack of response. One attempt at the Hanwell centre to consider losses associated with parenthood resulted in a group taking refuge in describing the pleasures of living in that area, with its village-like atmosphere, river and green fields. The leaders could not reconcile this description with their impression of the district and concluded that they were contending with a strong pressure to preserve certain images, however out of step they might be with reality.

The post natal meetings

The post-natal meetings, and particularly those which took place within three or four months of birth, were very different in character from those held during pregnancy. In contrast with the togetherness of pregnancy, the presence of the babies had the effect of fragmenting the groups, separating the marital partnerships and absorbing the attention of parents.

The disruption of the early post-natal meetings is conveyed by this recorded impression:

> A very difficult session to record. Conversations tended to be fragmented, unpursued, going on between several people at the same time, and the whole was punctuated by the noise of crying. The group did not work very consistently on any of the questions we asked.

The parents who attended with very young babies often looked exhausted and seemed to want rest and support from the meeting rather than anything more taxing. The leaders found they responded to this need in preference to pursuing what were, in any case, usually unsuccessful attempts to discover how marital partnerships had been affected by birth.

While change in marriage was seldom, if ever, the subject of discussion at these early post-natal meetings, a striking change took place in the way couples operated in the groups. Whereas in the ante-natal meetings the men had been active in discussion, this was very much less true once the baby was present:

> The whole session was taken up with the women sharing details of their experience of the actual births with each other and with us. The men were much more in the background. We got little or nothing about how it had been when baby and mother arrived home.

Occasionally, men would talk about how moved they had been by seeing the birth of their child, but usually they were quiet at the meetings. The preoccupation of the women with their own babies, and those of other mothers, presented the men who returned (and not all did) with a choice between involving themselves as quasi-maternal figures or opting out.

The back-seat nature of the men's involvement in post-natal meetings was replicated in the leaders' partnership. The one male member of the project team found himself wondering how he could contribute to the meetings and, sometimes, questioning why he was there at all. Similar feelings were recorded in another partnership between two women leaders:

> The conversation was mainly about babies with the health visitor very involved in the discussion. I managed to drag myself in twice—it felt an effort to do so and I was aware of breaking across the conversation and dropping things in from the blue. Both issues I raised (one concerned relationships with their own parents and the other the adjustments they had needed to make in the marriage) were related to well but briefly, and the conversation reverted back to the babies.

When change in marital partnerships was referred to, it was in the later meetings rather than the earlier ones. So, for example, this mother's baby was eight months old when she spoke about the pressure of coping with competing claims from baby and husband:

> Mrs Parker recounted an occasion when her loyalties had been divided. For weeks her husband had been wanting her to mend his jeans and complaining that she was too easily distracted by the baby. She sat down one evening determined not to be distracted until she had finished the patch. The baby started crying and she found her sewing speed increasing as she became more and more agitated. She went on to add that she does not take kindly to her husband's complaints that the interesting food they used to eat has been replaced by an endless repetition of ham and chips.

In a more positive vein, it was clear that husbands were important in providing access to a world beyond the baby:

> The women agreed that the return of their husbands from work was an important landmark in the day. It was a time to work towards, and if he were late for any reason it generated a lot of feeling. Often they would find they had nothing to say once their husbands were home, but just wanted to be talked to by an adult.

The demand on the men to replenish their wives' resources was lessened if there were other 'lifelines', as one mother described her access to friends and work. Yet the relative absence of reference to marital partnerships in the early meetings suggested that the implications of the baby for marriage surfaced, or at least were acknowledged, later rather than earlier. When most of the postnatal meetings were held (i.e. within six months of birth), the nursing couple (mother and baby) featured very much more prominently than the marital couple.

Having weathered the storm of birth, parents (and particularly mothers) were preoccupied with the baby surviving, and with surviving the baby. In this sense, the babies were capable of absorbing the attention of their parents by the magnitude of the responsibility they conferred upon them, and by their capacity to promote or undermine the confidence of parents in their new role.

The fragmented nature of the early meetings might be explained in terms of a lack of 'togetherness' experienced by parents burdened with an unfamiliar and weighty responsibility:

> Mrs Palmer had fed the baby during the night and had returned to sleep. She had then awakened thinking she had fallen asleep feeding the baby and frantically searched the bed for him. The first place she searched was under the pillow. The last place she looked was his cot, where he was fast asleep.

While the babies drew their parents' attention, they also attracted the attention of others to their parents. Their capacity for attracting attention could generate some competitiveness:

Mr and Mrs Mills arrived first with their baby in a carry-cot. She was soundly asleep and remained so throughout the whole evening in spite of Mr Mills uncovering her, rubbing her tummy, talking to her and, from time to time, giving the carry-cot a prod with his foot, muttering: 'Wake up and show yourself.'

In contrast, Mr and Mrs Stevens arrived with a wide-awake and slightly fretful baby who was passed happily between them and then to me. They were delighted when I held him at head level and talked to him and he kept up a gurgling 'conversation' with me (which only he and I could understand, of course!). I passed him back when I sensed some good-humoured displeasure from Mr and Mrs Mills that their baby continued to sleep and wasn't going to be shown off. 'Wake up,' said Mr Mills to the baby, 'you're letting the side down.'

At other times, a baby could attract unwelcome attention to his parents and undermine their confidence. In the following illustration a couple were contending with the inconsolable crying of their baby in the group and they found the experience very unsettling. Despite receiving support from the other parents, they did not attend subsequent meetings:

They said that in his waking hours their baby sometimes got beside himself with crying; they thought wind or colic was probably responsible for this. In the meeting they were painfully uncomfortable about the crying and ill at ease with their baby, holding him away and passing him between them. The health visitor took him off their hands for a few minutes to give them a break. Her steady and firm handling of the baby quietened him to the point of sleep. This seemed unbearable to the mother, who reclaimed him, with the result that he started crying again. After the meeting her husband approached me and was very critical of a television programme in which a doctor had demonstrated to a mother that her baby's crying was connected with her anxiety.

Putting the ante- and post-natal meetings together, a flow and ebb was discernible in the tide of marital partnerships as they appeared in the groups. During pregnancy, a closeness between couples culminated in the often moving experience of sharing the experience of childbirth. In the early weeks and months of parenthood, the central partnership was between a mother and her baby. Fathers were relatively absent from meetings held at this time (both physically and in terms of their contribution), as were explicit references to changes taking place in marriage. The joint preoccupation of parents with their newborn baby eclipsed the impact of parenthood upon marriage. Parents were concerned to hold themselves together as individuals at a time when they were experiencing important changes in their personal lives and were adapting to a greater differentiation and separateness in their roles and relationships than before; their partnerships were, in consequence, relatively inaccessible in the weeks and months close to birth.

EVALUATION

Mutual support

The couples who responded to an invitation to evaluate the groups, either at a meeting or by means of a postal questionnaire, were in agreement about the value of making contact with others who were in a similar position to themselves. Some written evaluations make the point:

> It was helpful to realise how other couples expecting a baby were feeling. We all seemed to have very similar worries and it was reassuring to realise this.

> It was good to speak to people who were at the same stage of pregnancy and parenthood, and to hear different attitudes to the same problems. It made me feel how important it was to do what you *feel* is right—to look inward as well as outward—to trust in your own judgement and learn from the experience. I learnt a lot about myself—not so much through what I said, but what I didn't say. It was the first time that I had ever been to an organised group and I got a great deal from it. The only thing I didn't like about the evenings is that they are not continuing.

> They were helpful because of sharing worries and finding others in similar situations. Discussing the problem made it more clear, even when perhaps the feeling was of guilt about wanting freedom from the responsibilities of being a parent.

> I found that they were helpful, not so much in their content but in their form. What we did discuss was not particularly original and interesting but it was nice to be with couples in the same boat as us, experiencing the same anxieties and problems. I became very interested in the other babies. I see them and the mothers. We are still in contact with all the couples. Afterwards we used to go to the pub and talk about everything but in a more relaxed way. All in all, very positive and enjoyable.

The leaders, similarly, were convinced about the social value of the groups for many of those who came. Contacts were made which were kept up after the meetings ended. It was striking, for example, that a follow-up meeting held at the Laurel House centre was attended by all but one of the couples involved in the two programmes held there, despite months having elapsed since they last met.

As important, the groups established a link between couples and the health visiting service. In many cases both husband and wife were given an opportunity to meet their future health visitor which they would not otherwise have had. Some health visitors commented to the project team that meeting couples through the groups had paid dividends in their subsequent work with families.

Leadership

Comments about the style of leadership were closely connected with how structured the groups were perceived as being. The form of the meetings was novel to some couples and evoked a mixed response:

Mr George said he was absolutely amazed at the meeting. It had been so different from what he had expected. They had come armed with notepad and pen expecting to receive a list of instructions from 'some old fuddy-duddy'.

His statement was two-edged in the sense that an expectation had been disappointed—there had been no list of instructions. The point was made more clearly by another man who

> . . . said that he and his wife had talked a lot about the group afterwards, but had not got the answers they were looking for. Because they had not appreciated the reasons why the groups were conducted as they were, they had felt critical of their leaderless nature. At the same time, he felt they had got to know other people in the group, and contrasted this with more structured classes attended previously where the relationship was with the leader, and with no-one else in the group.

While not behaving like instructors, the leaders were active in the discussions. They were often asked whether or not they were married and had children of their own. Those who were, and had, found that they were repeatedly drawing upon and sharing with the group their experience of becoming parents, while at the same time resisting pressure to turn them into experts who 'knew best'. They felt their experience was important as evidence that people came through the events and feelings which members of the group were facing. At the same time, the pressure upon the leaders to become involved in this way, and in that sense to become like other parents in the group, may have reflected a wish to deny differences and to preserve a sense of togetherness in the meetings.

The project team, like the couples themselves, were in an unfamiliar role and setting, and they, too, were often taxed about what constituted an appropriate contribution to discussion in their role as leaders. As one member recorded:

> They had, I think, enjoyed the evening, especially the men. However, I think we were not able to pick up the underlying anxiety and I am left wondering just how helpful they had found it. The health visitor's contribution was superb. Her friendly directness helped them to relax. I, personally, felt like a fish out of water. I kept finding myself holding back comments because they felt too much like an interpretation and I wasn't too sure how appropriate it would be to do that. On the other hand, at the end of the meeting I felt it was the missing bit.

Occasionally, there were suggestions that the leaders might have been bolder in their interventions:

> Mr Green said that with the advent of fatherhood he had thought more about death. His survival now seemed more important to him and his wife than it had done previously. He recalled having said something in one of the ante-natal meetings about wondering what sort of world they were bringing their children into. It had not been taken up by us, or anyone else, and had therefore been difficult to pursue.

There were corresponding occasions when the leaders had spoken out and received no response.

On balance, the project team considered that the discussion groups demanded too much of those who came, in terms of assuming responsibility for how the groups were to be used, at a time when their personal resources were being conserved. The prospect and reality of looking after a helplessly dependent infant is likely to increase the attraction, for parents, of dependent attachments. The success of the highly structured American programme of intervention described in Chapter Three (Gordon *et al.*, 1960) might be understood in such terms. This highly structured programme offered more certainty than the discussion groups described here, and thereby offered greater protection against the anxiety associated with the uncertainties of change.

It is, perhaps, relevant in this context to ask whether the drift towards medicalisation in the perinatal health services has its roots not only in an enthusiasm to apply the fruits of technological development in medicine, but also in the needs of prospective parents for certainty and assurance during a time of increased uncertainty and anxiety. The danger of an alliance between these two factors lies in depressing the capacity of individuals to draw upon their own resources, and in over-inflating the ability of the health services to manage. On the other hand, the programmes of group discussion may have weighted themselves too heavily the other way and in consequence afforded too little in the nature of a secure framework.

The group setting

From the observations of couples and leaders it was clear that the group setting placed limits upon how meetings were used. One man, in his written evaluation, put the problem in terms of protecting others from his anxiety:

'I found it difficult to bring up what really worried me because it did not seem fair to spread my own fears. I think other people might feel the same and then, perhaps, people's most important fears don't come into the open, but I don't know what you can do about this.'

Another man, at the final meeting of a programme, voiced concern about maintaining credibility in the eyes of other members of the group:

Mr Freeman said he and his wife had all sorts of questions which they would have liked to ask but refrained from doing so in case they were thought silly by other members. There was relief when someone else asked the 'silly' questions. Another member of the group commented upon how vulnerable people were in a group and therefore how determined to protect themselves. She had been a member of a group which had met for three years and there had never been the sort of openness that she experienced, for example, with a close friend.

From the outset it had been an open question as to how far, in a group, it would be possible to monitor changes in family relationships and to talk about the feelings these changes engendered. The problems of self-disclosure increase where marital issues are concerned. Allegiance to marriage may conflict with allegiance to the group, however much assurance is given that personal and marital privacy will be respected. The protection of marital privacy is particularly likely to override other allegiances at times when there is a need for togetherness in that relationship.

Even when marriage was not the issue, the leaders noted that parents usually felt they needed to be functioning in their new roles reasonably well if they were to expose themselves to the observations of others. For example, babies had to be relatively 'good' if their parents were to come to the meetings:

> One mother was telephoned by another member of the group to ask whether or not she would be attending the group that night. She said she would not be coming as her baby was 'bad'. The friend assumed she had meant 'ill' and expressed concern, but was then told that he was not ill, just fretful and naughty, and she could not bring a crying baby to the group. The friend had protested that a crying baby would not be excluded, but the mother had been adamant.

Couples were likely to say very much more about themselves when they were the only ones to turn up to a meeting, or when they had a chance of speaking to one of the leaders on their own, either before the others arrived or, for example, when washing up afterwards. In one instance, there was a sizeable discrepancy between the extent to which the couple had talked about themselves and the considerable worry they had been through with their baby when they were the only ones to attend a meeting, as compared with an earlier occasion when other couples had been present. In the group setting, they had described the early months of parenthood as straightforward; on their own they admitted just how anxious they had been. These indications that people are very much more accessible when approached on their own have important implications for health visitors in their contact with individual families.

Timing

There was evidence to suggest that the timing of the discussion meetings significantly influenced how much people could hear and acknowledge in the groups.

During pregnancy, it was uncommon for a selective deafness to operate in connection with issues which were at odds with personal preconceptions about parenthood. In a post-natal evaluation meeting one man illustrated this point:

Mr Dearman said that his only criticism of the parent group was that we hadn't given them enough preparation for the negatives—the tiredness, the disturbed nights, the need always to be on hand for the baby. We said we were surprised about this as we thought we had talked a lot about the 'losses' in having a baby and had wondered if we had overdone things. Mr Dearman looked thoughtful and said 'You're right. . . . I see now how difficult it must be to run this sort of group—there are some things we just don't want to hear and to know—and you can't *make* us hear them until we're ready.'

On other occasions it was clear that anxiety accounted for a wish not to hear. A mother at one of the ante-natal meetings made reference to an illness she had suffered during a critical stage of her baby's *in utero* development. This information made the leaders anxious for her, but she herself seemed to be untroubled by it. She went on to question the wisdom of rehearsing 'problems', and said she was sure she would manage birth without any difficulty. However, in an aside to one of the leaders at a later meeting she indicated that it was only after the threat to her baby had passed that she had allowed herself to know how anxious she had been:

> When she looks at premature babies now they give her the shudders, they look so small. Hers had been even smaller and lighter than they, but she hadn't worried at the time.

The indications that people may be more aware of, or more inclined to speak about, anxiety at some distance from when it is experienced most acutely, received support from material connected with changes taking place in marriage. In the following sequence, there is evidence of anxiety being acknowledged retrospectively, and current feelings being connected with previous causes:

Baby aged 7 weeks
Mrs Stevens had been in hospital for seven weeks prior to the birth. Mr Stevens had muttered, as his wife announced this, 'I could have lost my wife'. She, although older than the other women, was tonight little-girlish and very excited—I suppose a little 'high' would fit. He, however, appeared subdued and depressed.

The fact was that Mr Stevens *had* lost his wife while she had been in hospital. He could acknowledge some feeling about that retrospectively, but not in connection with his current loss of his wife to their baby.

Baby aged 12 weeks
He took up a question asked by one of the leaders about changes in the marriage, saying that he and his wife had been married for six years and had well outgrown the 'lovey-dovey' stage (to which she muttered a surprised exclamation); he went on to say that they felt like two separate persons with their own worlds as well as a shared one.

He thought the baby had *not* seemed like an intrusion and had not come between them. Mrs Stevens, however, brought the other side. She said she did get frustrated with the baby when he refused to settle and she wanted to be with her husband. . . . I found it was interesting that Mr Stevens led the discussion about separateness, because of all the couples in the group he and his wife were actually the most 'lovey-dovey'.

They were the only couple of their group to attend the final post-natal meeting:

Baby aged 22 weeks
He thought they would be telling a different story if he hadn't been invited to be involved in the birth of the baby prior to it happening, and he linked this to the invitations of the parent group and the National Childbirth Trust. He thought that had he not been invited at that stage he would have had difficulty tolerating the closeness between his wife and the baby during the first few weeks.

There were other instances as well. For example, the film *Sexuality and Communication*, shown at a post-natal meeting, was discussed afterwards in terms of how useful it would have been when couples had first been married. No reference was made to current sexual relationships, although it was only to be expected that some adjustment was being made sexually at the time. This is not to suggest that the relative absence of marital issues in the discussions can be explained solely in terms of an avoidance. It was clear when many of the meetings were held that parental preoccupations were more pressing than those to do with marriage, and it was in any case unlikely that sexual adjustment would feature prominently in a group which met only six times.

Comment

It is perhaps understandable that people in the throes of change may need to hold themselves together to survive, and may channel their energy towards getting through the immediate future with less recourse to others. If security is threatened, defences become necessary. There was evidence arising out of the groups which indicated that distance from stressful aspects of experience encouraged couples to talk more freely than when a threat seemed immediate or when other couples were present.

This challenged a theoretical foundation upon which the groups had been based. The assumption that people are more accessible during critical periods of change is central to crisis theory. Our finding that individuals and couples were less accessible when most anxious, and prepared to acknowledge disturbed feelings only when their immediacy had passed, raised a question about the usefulness of crisis theory in the management of predictable life events like the birth of a first baby.

While birth heralds an important period of change in the family, the project team considered there were two problems in regarding that change as a crisis. In the first place, crisis theory has traditionally concerned itself with response to an actual loss, such as bereavement. Although at the birth of a first baby couples may experierice a sense of loss, both as individuals and in their relationship together, it may take time for this to become apparent. When it does so, there is no bereavement in the sense of losing a life or a limb, only a process of disengagement which must be completed successfully if the new situation is to be adequately managed. Loss of this kind is neither immediate nor self-evident, and so does not permit the kind of socially sanctioned catharsis which accompanies visible loss. By encouraging the expression of feelings associated with loss as well as gain, the discussion groups ran counter to cultural as well as personal pressures.

Couples who attended the groups were normally those who had planned to start a family and they were more aware of prospective gains than they were of losses. In so far as loss featured in their thoughts, it was more the threat than the experience of loss with which they were having to contend at the time the groups met. The threat of loss may require a different coping mechanism from the experience of loss; for example, a drawing together in the face of a threat which has not yet materialised and may therefore still be averted.

Secondly, the assumption that birth was the critical point of change for marriage was an over-simplification in that it failed to take account of differences between couples which both defined the nature of the experience for them and the time at which they felt most under pressure. A demanding baby may indeed resurrect fragmented infantile experiences for his parents which may have a ripple effect upon the marriage. On the other hand, later stages of a child's development may be more problematic for them than infancy. The nature of an experience, and therefore the definition of crisis, cannot refer simply to an event, but must take account of the meaning of that event for the individuals concerned in the light of their past history and present circumstances.

This view of crisis implies a different strategy from that which seeks to educate people about important life events in advance. It suggests a need for sensitivity on the part of practitioners and other relevant people who are available to families at different points in the life cycle. Prevention in this sense is not about stopping something from happening, but about establishing a framework within which what might turn out to be a difficult experience can be managed creatively. This in itself is good preparation for future change, and underlines the Latin derivation of the word *pre-vention* which emphasises *that which comes before.*

In conclusion, the experience of an admittedly limited attempt to approach couples on a group basis suggested that effective preparation for the emotional and family implications of parenthood cannot rely solely upon imparting information. However, structured programmes of education may be attractive and useful to parents in providing a degree of certainty at a time when change threatens to disturb established patterns to relating to their personal worlds. Equally important, they provide a point of contact between parents, and between parents and the health services, which may be needed to encourage the setting up of 'preventive' relationships.

To be effective intervention must speak to the heart of experience by creating conditions favourable to communication. Some distance may be necessary before communication is possible. Groups may not provide the best forum, since they cannot easily take account of variations in the nature and timing of critical changes for individuals, nor can they command the degree of confidence and trust that is required and is sometimes possible through individual contact. Effective psychological preparation for significant life events appears to hinge upon the assimilation and integration of past experience, which is likely to be facilitated by the availability of trusted, pre-existing relationships. In this context, the contribution of the groups can be described in terms of having established, for some, a link with other first-time parents, and with the health services, which could be, and sometimes was, subsequently utilised. In the field of mental health, the establishment of, and support for such relationships is one important meaning of the word *prevention*.

CHAPTER FIVE

An Individual Approach

'But if I'm not the same, the next question is, who in the world am I?' . . . her eyes filled with tears again as she went on, 'I must be Mabel after all, and I shall have to go and live in that pokey little house, and have next to no toys to play with, and Oh! ever so many lessons to learn. No, I've made up my mind about it, if I'm Mabel, I'll stay down here! It'll be no use their putting their heads down and saying "Come up again, dear!" I shall only look up and say "Who am I then? Tell me that first, and then, if I like being that person, I'll come up: if not, I'll stay down here till I'm somebody else"—'but, oh dear!' cried Alice with a sudden burst of tears, 'I do wish they *would* put their heads down! I am so *very* tired of being all alone here.'

Lewis Carroll

Health visitors meet many Alices in the course of their work and are familiar with the mixed feelings which the need for help can arouse. They are relatively well placed to encourage parents to talk about what troubles them, and are in a position to make the first move by visiting families in the privacy of their home surroundings, thereby removing some of the limitations which affected the discussion groups described earlier. Yet communicating is not always easy. This chapter examines some of the opportunities, constraints and conflicts health visitors face in their individual work with young families as they appeared from a series of workshop discussions.

The broad conclusion drawn from these discussions is that health visitors could not be expected to engage readily with family stress unless they had a regular forum in which the effects upon them of working at close quarters with family feelings could be expressed and understood in their proper context. It was the view of the project team that a forum of this kind should be regarded as an intrinsic part of the service offered to families.

The workshops constituted such a forum. They were used by health visitors to discuss aspects of work which caused them difficulty. The cases discussed were, generally speaking, those which, for the presenters, highlighted areas of uncertainty about the health visiting role. Their uncertainty was connected with four areas of conflict in the work. Mediating these conflicts, in herself and in the families she visited, was an important aspect of the health visitor's role, and required of her an ability to tolerate uncertainty. As the project progressed, health visitors demonstrated a developing capacity for managing the conflicts inherent in their role.

While the workshops identified an area of professional need, it took time for sufficient trust and confidence to develop for open discussion of the members' work. Moreover, the contagious nature of family anxieties was capable of affecting how health visitors presented their work in the workshops. Health visitors could feel as helpless as the mothers they visited when their interventions failed to have the desired effect. They could be equally anxious to conceal their feelings. Their response to feelings aroused in the course of their work was crucial to the kind of help offered to people, many of whom were facing difficulties which were not amenable to ready solutions. The workshops provided a forum in which the response of health visitors to family stress was influenced.

THE WORKSHOPS

The workshops were set up as a forum for health visitors to discuss issues arising out of that part of their work which concerned couples who were starting a family. The task was to 'study the effect on the marriage relationship of a first baby and its implications for the role of the health visitor'.* The way families were presented to the workshops, the ability of members to carry out the designated task, the themes which recurred in discussion, and the light cast upon, and implications for, the role of the health visitor, form the substance of this chapter.

Two workshops were run concurrently over an eighteen-month period in which the discussion groups for couples were being held. The Mattock Lane workshop had a membership of eight health visitors drawn from that centre and the neighbouring Laurel House clinic. The Hanwell workshop (held at the Health Education Centre of a local hospital), had thirteen members, five of whom came from the Hanwell and Islip Manor centres. The remainder came from five other clinics in the area. Taking account of six withdrawals (in all but one instance because health visitors either changed jobs or left the area) and three replacements, a total of twenty-four health visitors participated in the discussions. The two workshops met weekly for one and a half hours.

Health visitors brought details of their day to day work with sixty-four families. *Whether or not these families were representative of a health visitor's workload or, indeed, whether they were accurately represented by her was not the primary consideration. It was assumed that the families would constitute as much a vehicle for the professional concerns of health visitors as data in their own right. Questions concerning why the meetings were used in the way they were, what determined the selection of cases for discussion, and which themes*

* The full prospectus appears in Appendix IV.

persistently recurred, were the important ones for the project's purposes. The variety of themes demonstrated the complexity of the health visitor's role in dealing with the wide range of factors which affect the capacity of parents to take up the challenge of their new responsibilities. Generally speaking, the families discussed were those with whom health visitors wanted particular help. The illustrations which follow should not therefore be taken as an accurate representation of their work as a whole.

THE ROLE OF THE HEALTH VISITOR

Official scope

As a result of their previous professional experience in hospital nursing and the historical development of the health visiting service as a whole, health visitors have deeply rooted medical connections which influence the way they perceive their role. As a community-based service with a preventive health function, health visiting can be traced back to 1862 when the Ladies Sanitary Reform Association of Manchester and Salford employed staff to visit all and sundry in their district, concentrating upon cleanliness, good living and giving advice about the care of children and sick members of the family. In statutory terms, things changed little over the next hundred years. The National Health Service 'Qualifications of Health Visitors' Regulations of 1972, which are based on the 1946 National Health Service Act, define a health visitor as 'a person employed by a local health authority to visit people in their homes or elsewhere for the purpose of giving advice as to the care of young children, persons suffering from illness and expectant or nursing mothers as to the measures necessary to prevent the spread of infection . . .'.

Recent definitions of their function reflect the accelerating process of change to which the health visitor's role has been and is at present subject. Merrison (1979) refers to a circular from the Chief Nursing Officer in the Department of Health and Social Security in which the health visitor is described as:

> a family visitor and an expert in child health care. She is trained to understand relationships within the family and the effects upon these relationships of the normal processes of growth and ageing and events such as marriages, births and deaths. She is concerned with the promotion of health and the prevention of ill health through giving education, advice, and support, and by referring to the general practitioners or to other National Health Service or statutory or voluntary services where special help is needed.

In his book *Primary Health Care,* Hicks (1976) reproduces Appendix 8 of the Mayston Report to indicate the enormous breadth of the official job description for health visitors as it now stands. He comments:

By the time I had finished copying out this very long job description I was grateful that the Lord's prayer was so short and the eleventh commandment shorter still. However, the exercise of copying was necessary. This is what the experts under Mayston's chairmanship tell us is the job of the health visitor. . . . My first reaction was that it was a cruel burden of responsibility to impose on anyone; there are nearly sixty separate items. I comforted myself by remembering that descriptions of most responsible jobs embrace many defined tasks. But by any method of counting, the above is a formidable list requiring a wide-ranging knowledge and rare gifts of presentation and persuasion.

Such a broad definition of role, spanning as it does the complete human life cycle in its medical, social and psychological aspects, wrestles with the complexities of adopting an integrated approach to the health and happiness of individuals in their personal surroundings. In this sense, health visitors occupy a potentially creative position. They also occupy a vulnerable position. Their vulnerability is evident in a booklet produced by the Health Visitors' Association (1975) which expresses concern about families, doctors, social workers, voluntary organisations and even researchers, envisaging 'health visitors as the ideal adjuncts to their own particular enthusiasms'.

It is perhaps understandable that, in response to this sense of vulnerability, health visitors have been anxious to maintain their clarity of purpose. Such clarity is not always easily maintained in the course of visiting. The evidence from the workshops supported the view that health visitors were subject to influences and pressures which had an important bearing upon their role, their behaviour, and upon how far they could afford to listen.

Family influences

While health visitors were predisposed towards defining their role in terms of physical health care (because of their previous professional experience and the historical roots of health visiting as a service), the workshop discussions suggested that many families were preoccupied by their emotional and social needs at the time they were visited. Discrepancies between family needs and the offers of help which health visitors felt able to make required mediation if an appropriate and effective response was to be forthcoming.

On the face of it, social and emotional needs appeared to be more accessible when families were approached individually than when they were approached through groups of the kind described in Chapter Four. In 43.8 per cent of the workshop cases, some marital stress was mentioned by one or more family members to their health visitor.

The hypothesis indicated by the discussion groups described earlier—that awareness of and willingness to acknowledge change in marriage occur later rather than earlier in the post-natal period—receives support from the overall figures. Among the 43 families with first babies aged one year or less when first presented to the workshops (see Table I, Appendix IV), the average age of the baby was 6.1 months in cases where explicit reference was made to stress in marriage, as compared with 4.4 months in cases where no such reference was made.

In terms of age and occupational groupings, the workshops' families also had much in common with those who attended the programmes of group meetings described earlier. The majority of mothers were relatively elderly: 55 per cent of first-time mothers and 59 per cent of the total group were aged twenty-eight or over (see Table IV, Appendix IV). Families presented were mainly from social classes II and III, the latter comprising the larger group (see Table II, Appendix IV). In occupational terms, health visitors are listed under social class III, so some affinity could be said to exist between health visitors and those who confided in them about tensions in their marriage. Alternatively, or perhaps additionally, it could be argued that health visitors required most support for cases which came 'closest to home', and this explained why they featured in the workshops. Although the numbers were too small to generalise from, there were some indications that families from social class III were more likely to confide in health visitors than those from other social groups (see Table III, Appendix IV). While affinity has been established only in social terms, it is reasonable to suppose that there may be fewer barriers to disclosure, yet possibly greater barriers to listening between like than disparate groups.

The fact that some families more prepared than others to talk about tensions in their marriage did not necessarily mean that they wanted or needed outside help. Yet at the time they were considered in the workshops, a high proportion (30 per cent of first-time and 61.5 per cent of other parents) were receiving professional help from members of the caring professions other than health visitors, general practitioners and hospital paediatricians—for example, social workers, priests, psychiatrists, and probation officers. That such cases were brought to the workshops indicated that they presented health visitors with the problem of how to respond to these situations appropriately and helpfully, and that the involvement of other agencies with the same families did not necessarily alleviate this problem. For most people, the need for help arouses ambivalent feelings and so it is not always easily satisfied.

The ambivalence of families about accepting help

Despite an apparent accessibility suggested by the figures, many of the families visited by health visitors, rather like Alice, had mixed feelings about whether or not they wanted to be helped. When they *were* clear about needing help, they were sometimes unclear about the sort of help they wanted and therefore about how they wished their visitor to respond. Their ambivalence was frequently conveyed through unspoken communications.

The two cases which follow illustrate the ambivalence of families about accepting help from their health visitor. In the first case, her help was apparently unwanted, while in the second she was appealed to with great urgency. The cases illustrate two sides of the same coin, and in each the health visitor was faced with the problem of how to respond to their conflict between wanting and not wanting her help. Equally important, the overt and covert communications in these cases suggest that families are capable of prescribing particular roles for their health visitor of which both they and she may be unaware, and which yet have major implications for wider considerations of her role.

THE SANDERS

Following notification from the hospital, a health visitor made several attempts to visit Mr and Mrs Sanders, a young professional couple who had recently had their first baby. In her presentation she made much of the physical inaccessibility of the family; their home had been hard to locate, there was no reply when she called, she had had to go back to the hospital to find their telephone number and it was with the father (who answered the telephone) that she negotiated a visit, arranging to knock three times to identify herself because the door-bell was not working.

When she called, Mr and Mrs Sanders were at home and a plump, healthy baby was asleep in an old-fashioned carved wooden crib. The health visitor had a very cool reception. She was left to make the running in the conversation and she felt she was picked up by Mr Sanders on any slight inaccuracies in what she said. He acted as family spokesman and espoused the Leboyer method of delivery. He said that his wife's delivery had been perfect and their one regret was that an eminent doctor had not been able personally to deliver their baby. Now she was home, he felt their daughter should come first and she was to sleep in their bed for as long as she needed. When the health visitor asked how that affected their sleep, Mr Sanders avoided the question and replied, 'If you have them in your bed from the word go, they don't score points off you later'.

During the visit the health visitor was inhibited by a sense of awe and 'heavenly tranquillity' (her words) which made her speak softly, not daring to disturb the peace. She felt relieved when the baby whimpered but she was immediately put to the breast. Mrs Sanders was full of milk and when the feed was over her baby looked gorged to the point of overflowing. Despite her uneasiness, the health visitor felt she could not risk questioning anything for fear of disturbing both the privacy and the perfect image of parenthood so powerfully conveyed to her. Moreover, she felt in some way that the tables had been turned during the visit. Mr Sanders had chided her about the fact that her own children sometimes still tried to wrangle their way into their parents' bed! She felt very 'put down' and criticised by him.

It is important to establish why this apparently harmonious situation might not be accepted at face value. The key lies in the anomaly between what the family were presenting and what the health visitor was experiencing. If things were so good, why should the health visitor be made to feel so bad? She was an able person with children of her own and did not normally antagonise the people she visited. Because her reaction was particular to this family, one can assume it was related either to their experience or to something they touched off in the health visitor. Most likely, a sense of inadequacy in matching the ideal was relevant to the experience of both.

The dialogue during the visit had been almost exclusively between Mr Sanders and the health visitor. She had been acutely conscious of intruding upon their lives, and had felt both irritated by being 'put down' and something of a failure in not being able to make a helpful contribution. On the assumption that her feelings reflected what remained unacknowledged in the family, two explanations can be advanced for what was going on. In the first place, Mr Sanders can be seen as communicating his feeling of being an intruder into his wife's relationship with their daughter. His apparent expertise on childbirth and family sleeping arrangements once the baby was home served to make the health visitor feel incompetent and as if she had little to offer, perhaps in much the same way as he felt in relation to his wife. That he felt his daughter was a rival is hinted at in the reason he gave for sleeping together as a family: 'so they don't score points off you later.' The message was unconscious in the sense that Mr Sanders was probably unaware of what lay behind his words. In this context, the health visitor can be said to have been experiencing some of Mr Sanders' feelings which he was not able to put into words.

An alternative explanation would see Mr Sanders not as making an unconscious personal bid to be heard by the health visitor, but as the spokesman communicating on behalf of his wife. Following this line, the health visitor can be said to have been experiencing the mother's sense of failure to match the high standards of care which she saw her ante-natal classes as setting. In these circumstances, the way advice was received by her during the ante-natal period may have hindered rather than helped. The demonstration of ample feeding which occurred during the visit can then be said to have served as much to support Mrs Sanders' wish to see herself as a good mother as it did to indicate her baby's need.

Subsequent evidence corroborated the view that an idealised image of parenthood had been fostered early on as a protection against a sense of disappointment and personal shortcoming. Two months later the health visitor brought the case back to the workshop saying how surprised she had been to discover that Mrs Sanders had delivered her baby under epidural anaesthetic. This was incongruous with the picture of natural childbirth which had been so forcefully conveyed to her at the first visit, but was perhaps congruent with the sense of pain and discomfort having been suppressed within the family. Yet she was reassured about the couple. Mrs Sanders was picking up the threads of her old life, returning to work on a part-time basis and taking the baby with her. The ornate crib had been replaced by an ordinary cot and the baby no longer slept with her parents. The health visitor was not worried that Mrs Sanders seemed to ask little of her, nor that she told of instances in which she disagreed with advice from the clinic, because these were indications that she had recovered her own way of doing things. Later she met Mr Sanders, who commented that things went better once people were free to accept some advice and reject the rest. As the Sanders recovered a less aggressive confidence in themselves, the health visitor correspondingly felt she had recovered her own role and was able to perform, in her words, 'a good role of basic health visiting'.

In this case, the crucial role for the health visitor was not to be the expert with all the answers but to be the parent who was found wanting. It was a role unconsciously determined by the Sanders. There were indications that by tolerating the accompanying feelings and not competing with the parents for the role of the 'good mother' she reduced their anxiety about not measuring up to ideal standards as parents and assisted them in establishing confidence in themselves in their new role.

THE HOPPERS

The second case was brought by an experienced health visitor who, while leaving her clinic, had been accosted by a woman with: 'You're the welfare lady, aren't you?' The woman, Mrs Hopper, had then asked to be visited later that day because of an urgent private matter. She declined an invitation to talk in the clinic and yet asked the health visitor to park her car around the corner from her house because the name of the Area Health Authority painted on the side might start the neighbours talking. The health visitor had misgivings about being called the 'welfare lady' and about being asked to visit a woman who lived outside her area, but because Mrs Hopper's house was nearby she agreed to call.

Later that day she found Mrs Hopper alone at home in her stark surroundings. The inside of her house was bleak and empty. There were two chairs and a table, no television, but a drinks cupboard noticeable because it was fully stocked and none of the bottles had been opened. Her two year old son cried on and off during the visit but commanded little of his mother's attention.

The health visitor was told by Mrs Hopper that she and her husband had not spoken for several days, following a row in which she had thrown his clothes out of the bedroom. What the row had been about was not clear. Since it had occurred, the couple had communicated only by note. That day she received a note from her husband (still living in the same house) to say that he would provide for their son but not for her. The difficulties between them were said to have lasted as long as the three-year-old marriage. Having talked about how dissatisfied she was with her marriage, Mrs Hopper went on to talk about her dissatisfaction with her mother, who seemed always to send her things she did not want. What she did want was not clear, and marriage itself was represented as thwarting her satisfaction because it had been precipitated by the conception of their son. In her eyes, it had therefore not been freely entered into.

The health visitor felt she was dealing with a very depressed and needy woman whom it was hard to satisfy. Her needs were communicated in a self-defeating way which had the effect of driving people away. Normally a warm and responsive person, the health visitor found herself withdrawing from Mrs Hopper. She described her function as that of 'a referral agency', an impersonal term she did not normally use. She suggested to Mrs Hopper that she visit the doctor, but this was not well received because she thought he would prescribe drugs which she would then be tempted to take all at once. The suggestion of approaching the Marriage Guidance Council also received a lukewarm response, because Mrs Hopper was sure her husband would not involve himself.

The health visitor had the distinct feeling that Mrs Hopper wanted her husband kept out of the picture so that she could get something for herself. But what it was that she wanted and from whom, were difficult questions to answer. The health visitor thought nothing short of 'a magic wand' would suffice. She wanted to withdraw because Mrs Hopper was not her responsibility, yet she felt caught by the extent of her distress.

The workshop members were impressed by the number of conflicting messages which were being communicated in the presentation. On the one hand, there was a stark portrayal of the depressed helplessness of Mrs Hopper, the bleakness of her surroundings, her complaints that her husband had withdrawn his affection, money and very presence from her. On the other hand, there were suggestions of resources which were not being used: her husband was earning a good income, their bank balance was more than healthy, and the drinks cupboard was full but untouched. Moreover, she seemed to want her husband kept out. In many ways, it seemed as if Mrs Hopper was wedded to her dissatisfaction, and her rejection of suggestions contradicted what she said about wishing things were different. By approaching the 'wrong' health visitor and eliciting a 'referral agency' response she preserved a distance analogous with the communication by note in the marriage. Both seemed to preclude the closeness or help that she consciously wished for.

The case was not reported upon again and so the outcome for Mrs Hopper was unknown. The dilemma she posed triggered a lively general discussion about the susceptibility of health visitors to role-casting pressures from families they visit. Why did the health visitor allow herself to be manoeuvred into the position of a 'welfare lady'? Were the letters emblazoned on the side of official cars responsible for inhibiting families from using their service, or were they a necessary protection? Was the name *health visitor* an adequate description of their function as they saw it, or was their role decided upon by families, irrespective of what they chose to call themselves? The boundaries which governed the interaction between health visitors and families were clearly crucial to their effectiveness.

Inherent conflicts

Boundaries, as applied to human relationships, have been described as 'rules defining who participates (in a relationship) and how' (Minuchin, 1974). If they are rigidly maintained they can immobilise relationships by severely restricting participation and limiting what takes place between people. Conversely, if they are too diffuse, the degree of participation may threaten to destroy the difference upon which a relationship rests its claim to exist. Appropriately permeable boundaries are therefore essential to effective relationships.

Professional boundaries are defined by role descriptions. To be over-rigid in defining the health visitor's role diminishes scope for involvement with, and therefore understanding of, families. Paradoxically, to be over-responsive carries similar penalties. However, exposure to the emotional experiences of families can be an extremely vivid and personal way of learning about them, always providing there is the chance of recovery. Recovery requires regular technical support from within the organisation.

The workshops were used by health visitors for this purpose. In the course of the discussions, four areas of conflict were highlighted in the health visitor's role: between integrated and partial approaches to families, between medical and social orientations, between prevention and treatment, and between 'good' and 'bad' parental images. Each area of conflict overlapped with the others. They were potentially creative but in the absence of support could be managed in a restrictive way.

THE CONFLICT BETWEEN INTEGRATED AND PARTIAL APPROACHES

Theoretically, health visitors are available throughout the family life cycle. They aim to cater for the medical, psychological and social well-being of family members. In practice, their attention has to be greatly restricted in scope. Within that scope, priority is accorded to families with young children. Three observations are relevant to the way in which health visitors offered a mental health service to families.

Firstly, in almost every case health visitors visited families only after their babies were born. The figures in Table V, Appendix IV, appear to refute this. In fact, the ante-natal contact recorded in that table refers to any contact (including telephone calls or the presence of a mother at ante-natal classes) with any health visitor (not necessarily the one who eventually assumed post-natal responsibility). The almost complete absence of an individual continuing link between a health visitor and a first-time mother spanning pregnancy and the early months of parenthood was further suggested by the fact that there were no cases presented in which a mother was pregnant except when a health visitor was already in touch because of a previous birth. For first time parents, the live-born baby was the requirement for an individual link between health visitor and family. From what health visitors have themselves said, the picture of almost complete absence of continuity of care by one person for the same family pre-and post-natally seems to be an accurate impression, however desirable such through-care was considered to be.

Secondly, the attention families received from their health visitor was concentrated in the early weeks and months of a baby's life and diminished from there on (see Table I, Appendix IV). From the peak period of the first six weeks, there was a declining graph of ages at presentation, indicating a declining availability of the health visitor to families as the event of birth receded into the past. This trend is of interest when placed alongside the hypothesis mentioned earlier which proposed that the willingness of parents to recognise and discuss tensions in their relationship increased with the passage of time. The accessibility of parents may therefore be increasing as the availability of health visitors is decreasing.

Thirdly, the member of the family to whom she most often chose to relate was the mother. That is not to say that fathers were not seen, and table V, Appendix IV, suggests a relatively high degree of contact with them. However, these contacts were not usually pre-arranged, they occurred by accident (in the sense that the men were at home during the day as a result of leave, unemployment or shift-work) and their presence was generally peripheral to the focus of the visit. Yet the figures are interesting since they suggest that fathers are more available than is often supposed.

From the discussions that the project team had with health visitors about their work, it often seemed that the presence of a man at home constituted a problem or impediment to the relationship between health visitor and mother. Generally speaking, there was greater comfort for both wives and health visitors if they met alone. A sense of unease or being caught out was sometimes mentioned if the husband joined an interview. These remarks made by health visitors underline the point.

It is not easy to feel free to talk to mothers if fathers are there—it is a woman's business.

I feel I am being observed when there is more than one person present.

It's important to see mothers on their own to get on a right footing.

I feel uneasy if I do not see mothers on their own at first and have to make another visit quickly.

A discomfort with three-way relationships is apparent from these remarks, as is an assumption that the proper function of the health visitor is to relate to mothers about women's business. Yet this was not always so. One health visitor recalled a husband sitting in front of the television and turning the sound up when she arrived to visit. She withdrew to the other end of the room to talk to his wife. After a while the husband rounded on them both and demanded to know what they were 'whispering' about. The health visitor managed the situation in such a way that subsequently it was he rather than his wife who contacted her when they wanted a visit. By proposing an exclusive relationship with mothers, health visitors may aggravate any sensitivity in families to the divisive effect parenthood may have within a marriage.

In so far as the health visitors who participated in the workshops were available primarily to the nursing couple in the early weeks and months following the birth of a baby, they defined their role in a way which tended to preclude their relevance as potential midwives to emerging family units. It may have been entirely appropriate that their role was restricted in that way, that they should, in effect, have acted only as proxy mothers to the mothers themselves. If that delineation is accepted and the indications are that it is not, since resources are directed towards training health visitors to take account of marital and family relationships, the fact remains that 'the ever so many lessons' of motherhood are learned within and sustained by a family context. To ignore that context is to ignore potential resources in the family which may then remain untapped. In a culture which seeks to avoid using the words 'parenting' and 'mothering' synonymously, an integrated approach to the family is a logical consequence. That is not the same as saying that health visitors should become family social workers, or that they should cease to regard mothers as their main point of contact with the family. The difference is one of orientation.

THE CONFLICT BETWEEN MEDICAL AND SOCIAL ORIENTATIONS

One of the reasons given by health visitors for choosing health visiting as an alternative to staying in hospital nursing was the wish to be more in touch with individuals and families, and to escape from what sometimes felt like an object-centred world, with its remorseless tide of bodies needing attention. Crossing the boundary between hospital and community represented movement from a more to a less certain world, and provided a greater degree of flexibility and self-determination about where lines were to be drawn.

However, the pressures of this less certain world were sometimes capable of breeding nostalgia for the nurse's uniform, an identifiable symbol which suggested an unambiguous role, carried status and afforded recognition to both training and skill. The past could beckon enticingly in the face of what one health visitor described as the pressures of being 'Jills of all trades'. The difference between hospital and community nursing was expressed by another health visitor in these terms: 'In hospital, patients either get better or die.' In the community, it sometimes seemed as if the problems of 'rotten awful families' persisted to the point of becoming their *raison d'être*.

In several of the workshop cases, it was clear that health visitors protected themselves by confining their role to the physical well-being of babies in a way which raised and left unanswered some important questions. The following is a case in point:

THE LASLETTS

A health visitor presented what she described as 'an ordinary case', in which she had been visiting a young couple, Mr and Mrs Laslett, who had produced their first baby six months previously. Pregnancy and delivery had been normal and her visit, ten days after the baby was born, had suggested everything was going well. Two weeks later she called on the family again and learned that their baby daughter had been crying a lot. Mr Laslett was at home when she called and he, rather than his wife, engaged the health visitor in conversation. In particular, he talked about how unprepared they had been for the disruption their daughter had brought to their lives, much as they both loved her. The health visitor learned from him that their sleep was being disturbed because the baby shared their bedroom and woke in the night. He was very active in caring for the baby, making up feeds for her and even supplying the dried milk from his place of work. The health visitor thought that in some respects Mr Laslett was behaving like the mother in the family.

Because of the persistent crying she stepped up her visiting and became increasingly anxious about not being able to find a remedy for the baby's fractious behaviour. At first she suggested they change the brand of milk they were using and that they no longer accepted supplies from Mr Laslett's work. When workshop members asked about Mrs Laslett, there was no information about whether she had attempted breast-feeding or what her attitude towards feeding the child was. This omission was unusual for a health visitor, but reflected how absorbed she had become in the problem of the crying baby.

The new brand of milk made no difference to the crying and so the doctor was called in to help. He prescribed medication to ease the child's digestion, although neither he nor the health visitor had any worry about the baby losing weight; if anything, she was over-weight. The only worry was the crying and this persisted despite medication. The milk became the symbol for what was disagreeing with the baby while there was no evidence to support this. Efforts were all geared to stopping the crying while no-one knew what it meant.

When discussing the case, the health visitor said that she had been made to feel very anxious by the baby's crying and her attempts to try to quieten her were related to her own feelings of helplessness in the face of a problem which would not go away. This sense of helplessness left little space in the visits to explore anything other than the *baby's* crying. Presumably, the Lasletts were also feeling helpless and desperate but these feelings were not related to by the health visitor.

Earlier Mr Laslett had talked about the unforeseen impact their daughter had made upon their lives. This subject had not been pursued. In the workshop discussion, members wanted to know more about the parents, but the health visitor said that, despite her frequent visits, she felt she did not know them well and provoked the group by referring to them as 'Mr and Mrs Average'. Details were pressed for which were not available.

It was as if the frustration the health visitor experienced was recreated in the group, only this time it was about the absence of parents (and particularly Mrs Laslett) rather than the presence of crying. When the case was last presented to the workshop, the problem had been eased for the parents by the prescription of night sedation for their daughter, who was by this time eight months old.

This case illustrates the inherent conflict between medical and social interpretations of the same piece of behaviour, and the risks of coming down too firmly on one side at the expense of the other. The health visitor was rightly concerned about the baby's health and took medical precautions to ensure nothing was physically wrong. Yet her medical orientation caused her to focus attention exclusively upon the baby and her crying. She saw it as an ailment requiring treatment rather than a communication by one member of the family on behalf of the others. The wish to 'cure' the crying by-passed an opportunity to support the Lasletts in understanding its meaning for them, which, if it did not directly diminish the crying, might at least have made it more tolerable, and thereby less incapacitating for the parents.

It was only in the workshop that the health visitor was encouraged to talk about *her* feelings in the case, to ask whether her feelings might be similar to those of the parents, and to reconsider her role in relation to the family in consequence. It required conviction on the part of the workshop leaders that a crying baby might mean something other than a physically ailing baby before other avenues could be explored within the family.

A similar conflict was evident in the case of Mr and Mrs Neal, an unmarried couple who, for convenience, used a married name.

THE NEALS

A health visitor asked the workshop how she might help Mrs Neal who seemed remote from, and did not play with, her eighteen-month-old son. Mrs Neal thought that something was wrong with the boy. She worried about his temper tantrums and what she saw as his retarded development. She feared both might be caused by a physiological defect which she associated with his large head. His destructive behaviour worried the health visitor, too: he had broken his parents' television and record-player, and he frightened his mother by catching his breath if she tried to intervene.

As a first move, the health visitor, in conjunction with the family doctor, referred the boy to a specialist. Medical examination found nothing amiss and the health visitor's concern moved on to 'how he gets away with murder'.

On this occasion the health visitor asked questions which gave her access to information about the family. It emerged that Mrs Neal had experienced difficulty asserting herself with her own parents. Her mother did not want her to leave home, despite the fact that she was then in her early twenties. The health visitor thought that her attachment to Mr Neal, and then conceiving a baby, were important in enabling Mrs Neal to make the break from home. Although the baby was planned, she had been unable to tell her mother this, knowing that she would disapprove. Instead, she explained the pregnancy as a contraceptive failure.

This surface acquiescence was repeated by Mrs Neal in her relationship with her husband and in her behaviour towards the health visitor. So receptive was she to suggestions the health visitor made that the health visitor began to worry in case her advice was taken too literally and uncritically. Yet she never knew quite where she was with this mother. Despite appearing to go along with suggestions, Mrs Neal always seemed to default on offers that were made to help her. For example, she would agree to attend a support group meeting for mothers arranged by the health visitor, and then fail to turn up. She would accept prescriptions from her doctor and not use them. These, and other forms of behaviour, suggested she had more of a mind of her own than she led people to believe.

The workshop became absorbed in discussing why Mrs Neal had such difficulty standing up for herself in a direct manner. From her reactions to her son there were indications that she was both frightened and fascinated by his destructive behaviour; certainly she was reluctant to intervene for fear of making matters worse.

The problem of Mrs Neal's difficulty in involving herself with her son can be approached in two ways. First, one can operate on a handicap model and assume that she *could not* play with him or involve herself with him because she did not know how to—because she lacked the necessary skills. Once it was known that there was nothing medically wrong, the health visitor's first attempts to help (by offering group support to her and putting her in touch with other mothers), followed this line. Second, one can assume that she *would not* become involved because of the anger he stirred up in her. One interpretation of her anxiety about damaging the boy, and indeed her fear that he was damaged, was that the toddler faced her with her own aggressive feelings. By failing to control him, she unconsciously encouraged him to act out the feelings that she turned her back on in herself. In these circumstances the therapeutic objective identified by the workshop members was to work with and legitimise the aggressive feelings which belonged to Mrs Neal. Her anxiety about the tantrums might then be lessened, freeing her to respond firmly to her son's unruliness, a response which was likely to assure him that he was not out of control.

Through discussion of the family and her own feelings about visiting, the health visitor gained an understanding of some of the emotional needs of Mrs Neal and her son. To respond to these needs required of the health visitor conviction that it was appropriate for her in role to do so, as well as confidence and support from her colleagues and management supervisors.

THE CONFLICT BETWEEN PREVENTION AND TREATMENT

In the same way that medical and social functions can be segregated to delineate a manageable professional role, so notions of prevention and treatment can be kept in separate compartments to the same end. The health visitor, by describing her function as preventive, faces the temptation of identifying a 'healthy' population as her proper responsibility, as against an 'ill' or problematic population which ought to be the responsibility of remedial specialists.

In Chapter Three, it was proposed that mental health described a state of balance, an ability to tolerate internal conflict and external stress without impairing an individual's capacity to participate in life. The promotion of mental health was associated more readily with notions of care and containment than with those of immunisation and cure. By fostering an awareness of the tensions within families which might otherwise have gone unnoticed, it seemed at times to health visitors as if the workshops made their work more rather than less difficult, and were concerned with illness rather than health. There was a wish that others would treat problematic tensions. The segregation of 'healthy' and 'ill' families was demonstrated by one group of health visitors in the workshop discussions. During the first term of meetings all but one of the families presented were in a state of acute crisis or were experiencing chronically severe problems. They were said by the health visitors not to be representative of their caseload as a whole, but were thought to highlight the dilemmas they faced in the course of their work.

The reluctance to bring 'ordinary' families, those to whom health visitors felt committed in their preventive role, was explained by the members in two ways. First, the workshop provided a forum for discussing work *problems*, and there was more investment in doing that than in reviewing non-problematic cases. Second, and more significant in this context, some concern was expressed about the dangers of creating problems for families where none had previously been recognised. It was as if there was an investment in protecting ordinary and satisfying areas of work from scrutiny. 'Healthy' families might then not be exposed to the contaminating influence of problems recognised only where they had become extreme, a message which, if sensed by the families themselves, might deter both groups from using health visitors to their full potential. Problems would go unacknowledged in families designated as healthy, and would be a cause for despair in those labelled as ill.

The proposition derived from the discussion groups for couples is relevant to this dilemma. There, it was proposed that prevention is concerned with containing tensions by developing a framework of trusted relationships to be drawn upon when they are needed. This view of prevention receives some official support. In the Merrison report there is a recognition that the health visitor's preventive function is connected as much with when she is available as with what she does.

> Health visitors are unique in the health team because of their contact with the 'well population'. They visit families on their own initiative in the absence of crisis and hence are often the first point of contact with the National Health Service.

It is not that the health visitor might forestall some illness or crisis and in that sense prevent it from happening, although that may sometimes be possible, but that she can be there before the event takes place, irrespective of its outcome. Her presence then establishes a link which, by virtue of its existence, is more likely than otherwise to be used in the future.

THE TENSION BETWEEN 'GOOD' AND 'BAD' PARENTAL IMAGES

It will be apparent from earlier illustrations that health visitors are sometimes required by families to experience what it is like to be in their shoes, and this experience may include feelings of frustration and failure. These feelings can conflict with the desire to make a positive and helpful contribution to the families they visit. The first of the two illustrations which follow suggests that a capacity to withstand a 'bad' parental projection can have a liberating effect upon health visitors and families alike.

THE BRENTS

A health visitor visited Mr and Mrs Brent, a couple who had had their first baby after ten years of marriage. Their well-established routine for living together had been shaken by their baby, who was ten days old at the time of this visit. When the health visitor called, the door was opened by Mr Brent, who wanted to know whether they had to be visited, and asked for her credentials before allowing her into the home. His wife was upstairs, and he insisted that she would not want to be disturbed, nor would she require further visits. The health visitor asked whether she might in any case introduce herself to his wife.

When she joined them, Mrs Brent was at first very outspoken about what she considered to be bad treatment from the hospital where her baby had been born. She contrasted the National Health Service unfavourably with private practice. As someone who had taken pains to keep fit and healthy, she had been dismayed that her labour had gone on for nineteen hours and that her baby had been delivered by forceps. She implied that the hospital was to blame for this. She told the health visitor that she did not believe in maternity benefit, rejecting that in the same way she rejected the medical care she had received.

Having said all this, Mrs Brent fetched a notebook in which she kept a detailed timetable of her day with the baby. She asked the health visitor to check through it with her. She said that without the notebook she would forget where she was with her son and was clearly struggling to accommodate him within her routine. At the end of the visit she turned to the health visitor in front of her husband and asked: 'Can you tell me why I don't love this baby?'

Whatever the reality of the care she had previously received, the determination to reject health services (the parent body in relation to expectant mothers) as bad care-givers made sense as a means of protecting herself against acknowledging the way she felt about her baby. Better to see them as uncaring than her. By staying with, and being (by virtue of her employment in the National Health Service) the 'bad' parent, the health visitor was given an opportunity to legitimise feelings which were causing this mother (and presumably her husband) such anxiety.

In the second example, it was evident that there was a cost to the health visitor for attempting to be the 'good' parent in the face of an unconscious determination on the part of a mother that she should fail:

MISS LEE AND MR LANE

A health visitor described how she had been trying without success to help a teenage couple, Miss Lee and Mr Lane, who had a two-month-old baby. They lived in over-crowded conditions in the house of Mr Lane's parents. Miss Lee was under the supervision of a probation officer because she had previously run away from home. The couple were not married, and despite their elaborate plans for a wedding, they failed to convince the health visitor that they would ever marry. Their joint preoccupation seemed to be with the difficulty of leaving home and separating from their parents, however bad they were described as being.

It was not just Miss Lee's parents who were presented in a bad light. Her in-laws were putting pressure on the couple to leave their home, the doctor had removed them from his list, and even the housing department withdrew their offer of a home once they discovered that Miss Lee had used her mother's name on the application form. Knowing how difficult it was to help this girl, the health visitor made special arrangements at the clinic to ensure she would have a friendly reception when she called. Despite her attempts, the clinic visits always seemed to go wrong.

It was as if strong endeavours were being made by the mother towards creating a situation in which no-one could or would help, thereby making it necessary for them to stay with Mr Lane's parents. In her concern to be helpful, the health visitor had responded to calls in the evenings and at weekends; she faced an impossibly de-manding situation which she found over-taxing. She felt angry and distressed at the weight and inappropriateness of the demands that were being made on her, fear of the violence she sensed in the family, and a burdening sense of inadequacy and failure at her inability to improve the situation.

These feelings can reasonably be said to reflect the experience of a young, relatively unsupported mother, alienated from her own family and over-whelmed by the demands of her new parental responsibilities. Rather than blame herself for not managing, others were blamed in her place. The more the health visitor tried to help her in being a mother, the more intransigent Miss Lee became. The cost to the health visitor of trying to be helpful was a growing anxiety about being taken over by the family. This was eased only when, during a weekend crisis, she telephoned the probation officer responsible for Miss Lee for help. He related to the health visitor's exhaustion rather than the family's crisis, and by doing so helped her to be comfortable with trying less hard and restricting the scope of her involvement.

MANAGING THE CONFLICTS IN THE HEALTH VISITOR'S ROLE

External supports

In the last illustration the health visitor was able to draw upon the resources of a probation officer to contain her anxiety about working with a particularly difficult family situation. While other agencies were involved in many of the cases discussed at the workshops, inter-agency collaboration of this sort was not frequent. Of the sixty-four cases presented, referral was suggested to the families in only three instances and succeeded in just one.

Health visitors, like the mothers they visit, often felt that at the end of the day they were the ones left 'holding the baby' of their problematic families. Perhaps influenced by their hospital experience, they sometimes felt unequal to the task of relating to general practitioners as their equals when it came to holding on to a different point of view about family ailments. On the other hand, they often felt unsupported by, and occasionally contemptuous of, the help they were likely to receive from social service departments or marriage guidance councils. Sometimes conflict between the professionals reflected issues fought about within the families they visited. Yet there were occasions when collaboration was both possible and effective, usually because of the initiatives taken by individuals towards others whom they knew to be sympathetically inclined towards them.

The workshops were themselves an exercise in inter-agency collaboration, and most of the participants found them valuable. Very few cases were presented from purely academic motives. Almost always, the health visitor was niggled by some incongruity in what she observed, or discomfort in her working relationship, which was expressed and elucidated in the course of discussion. In this sense, the project team assessed the workshops as having an important containing function for the health visitors who participated. The fact that meetings were planned on a regular weekly basis and were not convened to meet work crises in an *ad hoc* manner meant not only that anxieties raised by contact with 'problematic' families might be held, but also that there was space to become a little more aware of those who might otherwise have been assumed to be managing better than they were.

Internal supports

From the outset, the project team assumed that the ability to be an effective parent was positively influenced by an effective marital partnership. To the extent that health visitors see their function as one of parenting young families, this assumption is likely to hold good for them too. An important 'marriage' for the health visitor is her relationship with colleagues who have management and supervisory responsibilities for her.

The project team did not set out with an institutional brief, but in the course of their work it became clear that it was not possible to consider the development of a service, whether delivered through groups or individuals, without taking account of the organisational base from which it was to be offered. However desirable change is considered to be, there will always be institutional repercussions which affect how feasible it is and how far it will be sustained in the future. The following observations are relevant in so far as health visiting is concerned with the promotion of mental health in the family.

In the workshop discussions, considerable antipathy was expressed towards the depersonalisation of community nursing services following their reorganisation in 1974. Some health visitors said that among their reasons for leaving hospital nursing was the wish to escape rigid hierarchic organisational structures. They felt that community nursing was in danger of developing in the same way as hospital nursing had done. This view was expressed forcibly by one of the workshop members in a published article (Farnese, 1978). Because of the reappraisal of the health visitor's role which has been taking place in the past twenty years, the organisational requirements of community nursing are, themselves, likely to change.

An organisation in transition offering a service to families in transition raises interesting analogies. For example, many of the workshop reports portrayed mothers as feeling devalued, deskilled by, and sometimes alienated from, those who were in a position to offer them help. Similar feelings were expressed by some health visitors, especially those who were new in post (as were nearly half the membership of one of the two workshops). Comments were made about the 'Alice in Wonderland' nature of their organisation, referring to what, from one viewpoint, appeared as an inverted value system, in which fieldwork was devalued and success was characterised by promotion away from direct contact with families. An analogy can be drawn between these remarks and those sometimes made about topsy-turvy values held in society as a whole, where pressures upon mothers can encourage them to return to work in order to recover resources and a sense of status in place of the draining experience and devalued responsibility of looking after a baby.

To continue the analogy, health visitors were capable of regarding their managers rather as they suspected mothers regarded health visitors: someone who might inspect and criticise rather than support and develop their practice. To seek out a nursing officer for help implied an admission of failure, and there was not always confidence that the end result would be helpful. Sometimes the reservations of health visitors reflected the 'keep out' notices that families put up. This reflection of the client's problem in the relationship between worker and supervisor, and its implications for training, have been described fully by Mattinson (1975). It follows that supervisors have a responsibility towards health visitors which is, in some ways, comparable to the responsibility health visitors have towards families. In the absence of effective working partnerships, self-protective and restrictive habits are bound to develop. The institutionalisation of defences against anxiety-laden aspects of work has been demonstrated in connection with hospital nursing (Menzies, 1970), and social work (Mattinson and Sinclair, 1979), and it may well be a process which operates in community nursing, as well as in other organisations which have a responsibility for providing a caring service.

Given that the health visitor is expected to take account of medical, social and psychological factors affecting family life, there will inevitably be conflicts in her role, not least because she is exposed to the emotional influences of those she visits. In these circumstances, containment for the health visitor is a priority if she is adequately to contain family tensions. Containment for the practitioner requires a technical competence which is distinct from administrative ability.

The workshops provided containment over a limited period of time, and when they ceased, arrangements were made by some health visitors for similar meetings to be held on a regular basis to support them in their work, in one instance making use of a local marriage guidance council. It was interesting that while nursing officers were available to be consulted by their staff, they neither proposed themselves nor were proposed by the workshop members as candidates for holding responsibility for the technical development of the service. One of the dangers in this situation is that of management roles and values becoming divorced from those of practitioners. At present, community nursing management positions are held by people who have, at one time in their career, practised as nurses and health visitors. Promotion means that they no longer visit families. A divide is therefore created between those who practise health visiting and those who do not. This divide, if too great, can hinder the essential 'marriage' between a management which seeks to develop and support the primary task of an organisation (the provision of a service to families) and a fieldwork team who can articulate the framework of support that is needed for them to function effectively in their role.

From the workshop material it was abundantly clear that as well as exercising influence, health visitors were themselves susceptible to the influence of the families they visited. In administering advice, support and information they were not, and could not be, uninvolved outsiders, but were part of an interacting system of relationships. This made it impossible to consider their behaviour without taking account of a role-casting pressure emanating from the families they visited and from their professional setting, both of which were in a process of transition. These often conflicting pressures centred upon the health visitor as mediator between different worlds, generating tensions which needed either to be contained or defended against. The positioning of the health visitor between the worlds of infant and adult, the medical world of the health visitor's past professional experience and the social world of her families, and a world which sanctions prevention as opposed to one which expects treatment, creates particular opportunities. It also creates problems of identity and needs for containment which are in some ways analogous to those of parents who, in a different sense, are between worlds and having to cope with change.

CHAPTER SIX

Preparing Partnerships: A Reconsideration

. . . to have and to hold . . . for better, for worse; for richer, for poorer; in sickness and in health . . .

Solemnization of Matrimony 1662

Becoming a parent is a mixed experience. This is the conclusion arrived at by many couples who recorded their personal impressions of the transition, some of which form the prologue to this book. Parenthood is for better *and* for worse, enriching some aspects of life and taxing others in an often unpredictable kaleidoscope of experience. An awareness of the full spectrum of that experience, and a capacity to manage creatively the images and impulses generated by it is a sign of emotional health. An ability *to have and to hold* the life represented in tangible form by the newborn baby is the desired outcome for parents.

THE CASE FOR PREPARATION

There is a growing body of evidence indicating that parenthood is not always the fulfilling experience couples expect it to be. In Chapter One, the description of two marriages demonstrated that even wanted children can throw marital partnerships into disarray. Babies re-evoke in parents experiences and feelings from their past which can affect their capacity to behave as they might wish or plan in relation to each other and their offspring. Birth has a personal meaning for parents fashioned from their previous experience of relationships.

Birth also has a social meaning, as the research studies in Chapter Two make clear. Babies reorganize the positions which adults occupy and the relationships in which they participate. The impact of these changes is experienced more directly by mothers than by fathers, although the social and economic consequences have implications for both parents. An interaction between the personal and social meanings of parenthood determines how the transition from two to three is experienced.

The evidence suggests that while marriage is undoubtedly affected by parenthood, it is also capable of affecting the ability of parents to respond constructively to their new responsibilities. A secure marriage can enable the partners to manage the tensions and conflicts precipitated by children; it can help them to hold in balance different aspects of the experience, acknowledging both the gains and the losses which accompany change. It was the potential of marriage to contain stress, as well as its vulnerability to stress, which provided both reason and focus for the work described in this book. Marriage has untapped reserves for laying secure foundations at the beginning of the family life cycle. For this reason, the discussion groups, described in Chapters Three and Four, invited couples to consider how a baby might affect their lives. Similarly, the workshops, described in Chapter Five, invited health visitors to review their work from a marital perspective.

APPROACHING COUPLES THROUGH GROUPS

The discussion groups aimed to develop the capacity of couples to contain in a creative way the stresses and strains which are part of becoming a parent. They provided a forum in which personal implications of change might be antici-pated, discovered, and given an airing. They operated on assumptions which were described in detail in Chapter Three. Among these was a belief that healthy adaptation to change requires a rounded awareness of its effects and implications; opportunities to anticipate and worry, in a constructive sense, about the future; and space to come to terms with the loss of certain aspects of a familiar past. It was further assumed that change is likely to be less unsettling when experience more or less accords with expectation. Contact with others who have experienced or are facing the same event in their lives, and with the professional services, might realign discrepant expectations and establish rela-tionships which would be helpful in the future.

The groups were held at local family health centres, a potentially relevant focal point for those expecting or recently delivered of a baby. The centres have the additional advantage of housing health visitors who, with the exception of general practitioners, are the professionals best placed to provide continuity of care before and after birth. Yet for some, health centres are alien territory. Studies outlined in Chapter Three indicated that a combination of social and psychological factors might result in a low rate of response to the offer of dis-cussion groups.

In the event they were right. Overall, the response rate was low, adding weight to the view that demand for ante-natal services is not self-evident. Yet within the overall figure there were some differences. Small health centres were more adept than their larger neighbours in fostering demand. Health visitors working there were better placed to offer personal invitations to the groups, and since they were normally directly involved as leaders, they had a personal investment in the success of the groups and firsthand knowledge about their purpose. The understanding between health visitors and the project team about the nature of the groups affected how they were described to couples when invitations were made. That understanding took time to develop and was best established between those who directly shared in the experience of running the groups.

The couples who responded to the invitations tended to be middle-class, professionally employed and in their late twenties or early thirties. They usually attended as couples, which suggests that men in this socio-economic bracket will respond to programmes whose purpose directly involves them. Social classes IV and V, where vulnerability to transitional stress is greatest, were unrepresented at the groups. No doubt social factors influenced the degree of comfort in, and perceived relevance of, discussion groups held at health centres. Psychological factors are also relevant. It was these which interested the project group and about which something was learned from the couples who participated in the scheme.

For example, there was a marked difference in the nature of the groups before and after birth. Pregnancy was characterised by togetherness, displayed between couples and reflected not only in the social homogeneity of the groups but also in a consensus of views articulated. Those who came experienced discomfort with differences, both in the groups and between partners. Often the idea of a baby, or the couples' ideas about themselves as parents, would act as a unifying bond. These ideas were not easily dislodged. A selective deafness sometimes operated in relation to ideas and information which might disturb preconceived images of parenthood. It was as if these images served as an organising principle in the face of future uncertainty, and were therefore not lightly to be given up.

The presence of babies in the post-natal period had the effect of fragmenting the groups, preoccupying the parents, and highlighting an important differentiating factor in the marital partnerships—there could be only one mother. The early weeks and months of parenthood, as reflected in the groups, overwhelmingly featured the relationship between mother and baby. Only later on (and after the first four months of the baby's life) were there occasional references to changes in marriage. This suggested that such change, as more than a temporary phenomenon, became apparent later rather than earlier, and that it could only be acknowledged retrospectively. In relation to anxieties about surviving the baby and the baby surviving, and in common with a pattern evident in the pre-natal period, worries tended to be referred to only when a crisis was past.

The fact that couples met in groups compounded the difficulties associated with self-disclosure. Personal confidences were more likely to be shared with the leaders outside meeting times, or when no other couples were present, than when the groups were in session. Privacy needed safeguarding. The response to the questionnaire described in Appendix I supports this view. There was more freedom to describe experiences and reactions in an open way given the protection of anonymity than was possible in the groups (although some couples who participated in the groups did identify themselves in their replies to the questionnaire). The replies were, in most cases, completed well after birth. In some cases, the respondents' children were by then more than a year old. Parents were usually, but not always, writing about an experience they had come through rather than one which they were currently experiencing. There were, then, indications that some preliminary private work had to be done before experience could be shared, and that experience was more likely to be shared with an individual, or with the protection of anonymity, than within a group.

The unstructured nature of the groups provided some opportunities and inhibited others. For those who came, the informal contact with others in like circumstances was the most appreciated aspect of the discussion groups. For the health visitors who participated, the chance to meet both parents during pregnancy was valued, and this affected their subsequent relationships with families in a positive way. Yet for all concerned, it would have been more comfortable to have adopted a teaching approach in the groups, thereby reducing uncertainty about what might happen at the meetings and demanding less of couples in the way of active participation. This suggested a wish for certainty in the face of change and a framework for tackling the unknown. The management of that wish, by couples and by services which make a response, is a nicely balanced issue. Too much certainty on the part of services induces a dependency which does nothing to muster the personal resources needed once a baby is born. Too little certainty, especially in areas where it is possible to make assertions (as in classes which offer education about various aspects of pregnancy, childbirth and parenthood, and which encourage rehearsal in these areas) removes a much-needed structure of support.

Given the limitations upon what could be done in groups, the workshops examined some of the opportunities open to and constraints upon health visitors in their individual work with families.

APPROACHING COUPLES THROUGH THEIR HEALTH VISITOR

It was clear from many of the cases presented by health visitors at the workshops (described in Chapter Five) that, as a professional group, they are well placed to help those they visit. Their links with young families in the early months of parenthood provide opportunities for assisting with the tasks of learning a new role and integrating experience, work which the discussion groups were able to promote in only a very limited way. Their help was often greatly appreciated by families. The cases selected for the workshops tended to be those which

highlighted the problems they faced in carrying out their work, especially problems associated with reconciling their role with the social dimensions of family
life in which the project team was primarily interested.

From case material, it was clear that the ambivalent bids made by some
mothers for the attention of health visitors could meet with an equally
ambivalent response. Caution against too much involvement between families
and health visitors was justified in terms of maintaining an appropriate professional role and protecting against an overwhelming claim on resources. What
constituted an appropriate professional role was by no means clear. Official
delineations encompass a huge field and so afford little protection to health
visitors, who are expected to be available to families throughout the life cycle
and to take account of medical, social and psychological factors in the course of
their work. 'You're anything anyone wants you to be,' commented one health
visitor, illustrating just how vulnerable she felt at times. This vulnerability
stems in part from the conflicts which are inherent in the health visitor's role.
Managed well, they can stimulate a thoughtful response and result in an
integrated service to families.

Like most practitioners, the health visitors we met experienced conflict
between the desirable and the possible, the desirable in their case being an
integrated through-care service for couples who must adapt to the arrival of a
new family member. For sound practical reasons their efforts were concentrated
in the early weeks and months of parenthood and aimed to help mothers to
adjust to their new role and responsibilities. Yet it was found that, in preparing
for this task, health visitors had only very occasionally met, during pregnancy,
the mothers whom they subsequently visited. The advantages they associated
with ante-natal contact and continuity of care were seldom enjoyed. At the
same time, it was not uncommon for health visitors to be faced with the legacy
of a client's unsatisfactory experience in the hands of others.

Because a mother's ability to cope with her baby depends not only upon
mastering certain practical skills, but also upon her state of mind (which is, in
turn, significantly affected by those around her), health visitors receive training
in helping people with emotional problems. Several of those who attended the
workshops were sent on courses intended to help them respond effectively to
marriage problems which became evident in the course of their work. In
practice, while health visitors were prepared to offer help directly to mothers,
they were much less comfortable with enquiring about or mobilising the
resources of a marriage. On some occasions they unwittingly made it more
difficult for a husband to involve himself as a parent and partner. Moreover,
while the workshops provided confirming evidence for the discussion group
hypothesis (that people are more willing to acknowledge emotional stress and
strain in their relationships as time elapses after birth), this potential
accessibility was matched by a declining availability on the part of health

visitors, who were generally scaling down their visits after the first three to six months of a baby's life.

In the face of social and psychological issues, health visitors were called upon to respond in a way which discounted neither the needs of family members (for example, by declaring emotional issues outside their province and suggesting referral for specialist help, which might not be wanted or needed), nor their own field of professional competence. Under pressure, there was a temptation to deal with the dilemma by limiting the scope of their involvement to the medical health of the baby and regarding emotional and social stresses as the responsibility of other agencies. 'We're not trained to deal with these situations,' said one health visitor. 'I can't believe I'm being of any help other than listening,' said another. The wish to act sometimes took precedence over the need to listen.

If there is one word used to define the nature and degree of a health visitor's involvement with families, in other words to define her professional role, it is *prevention*. Yet the distinction between prevention and treatment was by no means clear in the workshop cases. Nor is it a clear-cut distinction in the field of emotional health generally. Here, prevention is regarded as a graded response to deteriorating levels of infirmity. The distinction between health and illness is at no point clear cut, and definitions of either state will rest upon the attitudes of those making a diagnosis, social definitions of what is tolerable in terms of behaviour and condition, as well as the actual state of the person concerned. At its most extreme, the delineation of a preventive function invites an over-clear distinction between a healthy population, which is the proper client-group for health visitors (a group which would then logically need her least) and a sick population, which ought to be the responsibility of remedial specialists.

At this extreme, the definition of professional role in terms of prevention can approximate a professional myth, similar in some respects to myths which have been written about in the family. These have been defined as beliefs which support 'patterns of mutually agreed but distorted roles which . . . members adopt as a defensive posture and which are not challenged from within'. Such roles 'provide a useful blueprint for social action but at the same time . . . reduce . . . flexibility and capacity to respond to new and unrehearsed situations' (Byng-Hall, 1973). When this happens in a professional context the strategic advantage enjoyed by health visitors is severely undermined.

The unquestionable asset that health visitors possess is their station between worlds. They operate between the world of medicine in which they first trained, and the social world of the families they visit. They can relate to 'sickness' in 'well' families without converting them into patients. They are there for the 'well' population, and the 'well' population has problems. The potential to engage with sickness in health reduces any tendency to divide the world into 'good' and 'bad' families, a judgement which echoes that of the infant in his attempt to deal with conflicting experience, and a judgement to which parents are so often themselves susceptible. This location between worlds explains why the health visiting role is difficult to define in precise terms. The workshop experience suggested it could be seen as a mediating role, assisting families to change by integrating the emotional and physical health of individuals and relating to individual stress in a family context. Defined in such terms, it requires of health visitors a developed capacity to manage uncertainty, in themselves and in those whom they visit.

IMPLICATIONS OF THE GROUPS AND WORKSHOPS FOR PREPARATIVE AND PREVENTIVE SERVICES

The discussion groups for couples were based on two models of intervention. The first of these was the medical model of prophylaxis, already drawn upon by analogy in psychoprophylaxis for childbirth. Psychoprophylaxis assumes that rehearsal, and information disseminated during pregnancy, can act, rather like an immunising agent, to ease childbirth and prevent complications. The analogy was extended to the discussion groups. It was hoped that by providing a forum for couples, in which expectations and experiences could be shared, the risk of a prolonged and painful period of adaptation to change would be reduced and the health of the emerging family unit positively promoted.

The experience of running discussion groups called into question the usefulness of the prophylactic model in connection with the process of preparing for the emotional impact of parenthood. In relation to some information, the mind was capable of erecting barriers to the serum of knowledge. The problem was more complicated than closing the gap between expectation and experience because of an emotional investment in maintaining certain images of parenthood. Indeed, for some, expectations only became apparent after they had been disappointed. The indications were that the personal meaning and implications of parenthood could not be learned in advance but had to be discovered through experience. In the meantime, preconceived images of parenthood served to provide a way of imagining what, at the time, was unknown. These images could be censored to exclude aspects of life with a baby, or within the marriage, which might generate anxiety. Censorship was not readily lifted by information which presented different images.

The second model drawn upon by the discussion groups was that of preventive intervention. Developed in the mental health field and resting upon crisis theory, this model proposes that limited intervention close to critical periods of change can have a particularly fruitful outcome. In planning the timing of the groups it was assumed that, amongst the cluster of crises associated with parenthood, birth was a watershed. Intervention timed immediately before and after birth was expected to assist in the process of establishing a new and healthy family equilibrium.

Yet the findings of the discussion groups suggested that birth was not necessarily a critical turning point for marriage, and that crisis theory was neither as helpful nor as relevant to the process of intervention in relation to becoming a parent as had previously been supposed. Parenthood involves significant gains, and in so far as loss was acknowledged in the groups, it was the threat of losing an anticipated gain (the baby) which predominated over experiences of actual loss. At such times, when survival is threatened, perhaps a different coping mechanism is required, one which can mobilise defences and fight. When feelings of loss or anxiety were disclosed, some privacy, distance, and a reasonably secure sense of self were necessary preconditions.

Neither prophylaxis, with its implications that dis-ease can be avoided through the dissemination of information, nor preventive intervention, which assumes an accessibility to people at times when they feel most in disarray, provided adequate models for the approach to preparation attempted through the discussion groups. The personal meaning of parenthood had to be discovered through experience, and disclosure of that experience followed rather than accompanied its passage. Such disclosure was preparative in the sense that the integration of experience can be expected to equip people to handle change in the future more effectively.

The value of the groups was in helping to construct a network of relationships, with other couples and with the health services. Establishing a network of this kind is in itself likely to be good preparation for an uncertain future.

Simply because it is not possible to know exactly how parenthood will affect the lives of individuals and their relationships, it is not possible to know if and when they will require outside help. Developing a safety net is an appropriate task for health services and constitutes a preventive measure. Prevention, in this sense (as in its Latin derivation), emphasises that which comes before—precedence over deterrence. In times of need, services which have already established a link with families are more likely to be used than those which have not. It is, then, not just marriage which requires preparation, but the partnerships between couples and the services which may be in a position to help them at some later time.

This conclusion is drawn from a limited piece of practical work with a particular orientation and set of objectives. Despite these limitations, three questions are relevant to the strong case for parenthood preparation (and, indeed, preparation for other important events, like marriage itself) which has been made in recent years. In the first place, if preparation is to mean more than developing a technical competence in meeting the practical demands of a new role, what does the word mean when people experience events in so many different ways? Secondly, when is the best time to prepare people for different events in their lives? Can adolescents, who are emotionally preoccupied with leaving their parents, be expected to be receptive to programmes which encourage them to anticipate a time when they will themselves become parents, or does there need to be a matching preoccupation for such education to be effective? Thirdly, why is there so little take-up of preparation schemes when a need for them can be readily identified? Is the problem simply one of short-term lack of awareness on the part of consumers, which can be remedied through promotional activities, or are there more deep-seated issues which bear upon the protection of individual privacy or the wish not to accept change? In connection with this last question, it is interesting to speculate whether employment legislation, which encourages mothers to truncate their apprenticeship to motherhood through pregnancy and to hold on to the prospect of returning to work once the baby is born, reflect a wish to deny the change a baby brings and to avoid the wider social implications if motherhood is not to become an isolating and depressing experience.

The work described in this book answers these questions in terms of the importance of developing partnerships between services and the families or individuals who may approach them at different points in their lives. Continuity in service provision, and making links with potential users before services are required, prepare the ground for the effective containment of experience.

Continuity of this sort is rarely experienced by those who are starting a family, except when a general practitioner takes an active hand in the process. Since most babies are born in hospital, it is common for one group of people to offer a service during pregnancy (nurses, registrars, appointment secretaries, midwives, health visitors, ante-natal class teachers, consultant obstetricians and dieticians, for example) and for another group to take over in the early months of parenthood (notably midwives, health visitors and general practitioners). The break in continuity coincides almost precisely with birth. While the constellation of roles may remain stable before and after birth, the people in those roles change, and opportunities for developing a relationship in which there is trust and confidence may be few and far between.

Health visitors occupy a prominent position among those who might offer a continuous service. Not only are they available before and after birth, but also their role attempts to grapple with the complexities of offering an integrated service to families. To operate effectively in that role demands of health visitors a capacity to manage tension and uncertainty.

In order to tolerate stresses associated with their role, health visitors require a structure of containment geared to their professional needs, not dissimilar to that which has been advocated for the families they visit. They require 'husbanding' in their own right, in order to be free to involve themselves with families without fear of losing their professional identity in the process. This was the type of relationship which developed with the project team through the workshops. In a busy working week, these meetings provided an opportunity to discuss work crises and to review work which was not causing immediate concern—itself an important preventive measure. In this forum a climate of trust developed which allowed those who participated to acknowledge feelings of perplexity, frustration and failure without undermining their professional confidence. Generally, the workshops were regarded by health visitors as useful in their work and, as a group, health visitors showed an ability to develop sensitivity to the feelings of family members as they communicated themselves in different ways.

The obvious question which follows is what supervision and technical support is available to health visitors from within their own organisation? Upon the answer to this hangs the feasibility of the service responding in role to families in a way which takes account of medical, social and psychological factors. Supervision is available to health visitors, but in Chapter Five there was some discussion about factors which influenced whether and how that supervision was used. Parallels were found to exist in that respect between health visitors and the mothers they visited. In connection with psycho-social aspects of the health-visiting role, there tended to be agreement between health visitors and their managers that supervision was the province of outsiders. For example, when the workshops came to an end and there was a wish to continue the meetings in some form, it was thought more appropriate to approach a marriage guidance counsellor and a local authority social worker to convene the meetings than to designate a health visitor or nursing officer to this role.

It may be that health visitors and their supervisors share a fear of being found wanting in the grey areas of their role which encompass the social and psychological health of families. Health visitors expressed the view that they were more likely to approach colleagues than nursing officers for help not only because of their accessibility but also because they then ran less risk of being considered unable to cope by those who exercised oversight. Alternatively, they questioned whether their problem would be understood. No doubt a hangover from earlier hospital nursing experience coloured this perception. As one health visitor reminisced: 'If you reported sick, then you were either sent to the obstetrician or the psychiatrist!' Either way, there was a fear of losing professional autonomy as a result of consultation, a fear confirmed on those occasions when nursing officers reported to case conferences with other agencies about families with whom they had no personal contact and on behalf of the health visitors who were directly involved. While health visitors might find relief from public accountability through this system, and perhaps have an unacknowledged investment in nursing officers shouldering responsibility in such circumstances, supervision is hard to accept if the cost of exposing work is feared to be loss of autonomy and responsibility.

On the other hand, if nursing officers or others with supervisory responsibility feel they ought to have ready answers for their staff and be prepared readily to assume responsibility in cases which are causing anxiety, they might well hesitate before committing themselves to this task. Good supervision is the product of a lively interaction between the supervisor and the person supervised. One way for supervisors to keep in touch with the problems facing their staff is to carry a small caseload themselves. Another is for health visitors to develop a career structure which remunerates experience in practice, and to give experienced practitioners training responsibilities for their colleagues. Either way, effective work with emotional problems rests upon a capacity to tolerate distress and uncertainty, a capacity which, in turn, relies upon a working partnership between practitioners and supervisors which enhances and does not reduce professional autonomy.

It is also worth raising a question about the purpose (whether consciously conceived or not) of externalising some aspects of professional training. Might this practice serve to maintain the service as it is, in the face of changes which threaten to alter its character? Health visitors sometimes said that when their work involved them in counselling people with emotional problems they thought they no longer had the sanction of their organisation. This despite the training investment made by their managers in courses which fostered such skills and, indeed, their decision to host the project! If health visitors protect their supervisors and managers from the psycho-social implications of their work, and supervisors direct their staff outside the organisation for training in this area, it can be argued that different levels of the organisation collude, in order to avoid responsibility for grappling with the institutional implications of this dimension of the health visiting role. Creative containment has a structural aspect: sandwiched between midwives and social workers, health visitors need a containing organisational framework if they are to straddle the medical and social worlds of the families they serve.

With this broader view, preparation for parenthood involves more than alerting couples to the likely effects of children upon their marriage. There is a limit to the usefulness of information for parents, although imparting information provides a reason for couples and services to meet. Preparation for the emotional impact of parenthood means establishing relationships which can be called upon later as an aid to integrating experience once that experience has been lived through. The partnership between parents is not alone in requiring preparation. Partnerships between families and the services available to them need to be established before they are required. In addition, the partnerships within the relevant helping agencies will affect the ability of those directly in touch with families to provide an integrated service. In all three contexts, the containing relationship can serve as midwife to the emerging family unit, enabling those involved both to have and to hold the new life generated by birth. Developing such relationships is a proper objective for preparative and preventive services.

There is no birth without pain, no change without impetus to change. Partnerships require preparation, not to suppress the labour pains of a new era but in order that the transition can be lived, experienced and accomplished creatively.

APPENDIX I
The Questionnaire

Some observations

Early in 1979, 254 couples were sent a letter and questionnaire which invited them to describe their experience of becoming parents. In particular, they were asked how their marriage had been affected by the birth of a baby. They were told that our intention was to compile a booklet from their replies which might help other prospective parents. The couples lived in an area of London served by four family health centres, and they were contacted through health visitors from those centres. All had become parents for the first time in the preceding fifteen months.

While the point of the exercise was to collect first-hand accounts which would articulate a variety of experience, and not to identify normative patterns of response, some general observations about the replies are of interest.

Firstly, the respondents were mainly women. Fifty-seven replies were received from one or both partners of the marriage. Of the 26 replies received from one partner, 25 were from women. While the remaining replies were ostensibly from couples, only 10 out of 31 were completed separately by husband and wife. In many of the remaining 'joint' replies it was clear that the wife had acted as scribe, if not sole respondent.

Secondly, a high proportion of respondents described a temporary disturbance in their sexual relationship; 33.5% made explicit reference to some sexual dissatisfaction during pregnancy, as compared with 58% who did so in the post-natal period, although partners were not necessarily, or even usually, held to blame.

Thirdly, a marked change in the wife's relationship with her mother was frequently mentioned. This change was usually for the better, and in 49 per cent of the replies (the figure rises to 54 per cent if the relationship with the husband's mother is taken into account) specific reference was made to an improvement. However, in the ratings of those likely to be approached to alleviate emotional upset, parents came well below spouse, friends or even professional services.

The questionnaire was a demanding one, and in view of this the response rate (more than one in five) was better than expected. As promised in the covering letter, a draft version of the collected comments was sent to all those who received a questionnaire.

The covering letter

You will have been invited to, and may have attended, some evening discussion meetings for couples expecting their first baby. One of the intentions of these meetings was to tap first-hand experience with a view to compiling a readable booklet which would be helpful to other new parents.

The booklet will focus upon how *the relationship between parents* is affected by and changed as a result of pregnancy, birth and parenthood. It will consist of what people themselves say about the experience, edited into a presentable form.

Ideally, we would have liked to visit and hear directly from everyone who was invited to the discussion meetings, but this will not be practicable because of the numbers involved. As an alternative, we are enclosing a reply form in the hope that you will feel able to contribute something of your experience by this means.

We do appreciate that the reply form asks a lot, but hope you will feel able to respond, however much or little you want to say, as a help to future parents. The question headings are simply guidelines and should be disregarded if unhelpful. If you prefer to be visited, do let us know.

We have no way of identifying you with your reply form and anonymity is assured. At the same time, you should only reply if you have no objections to your comments being made public as part of a booklet. A stamped addressed envelope is enclosed for your use. Copies of the draft booklet will be sent to all who receive this letter.

Should you have any queries, we will be happy to answer them at the address and telephone number heading this letter.

With good wishes,
Yours sincerely,

Reply Form

Two forms are enclosed in case you wish to reply separately. Would you tick whether this form has been completed by:

husband

wife

both

Is your baby:

over six months old

under six months old

If you find it difficult to fit your comments to the question headings, please feel free to abandon the reply form and write what you want.

Should you choose not to use the form, or if you decide not to reply at all, we would like to know why this was if you are able to tell us. Question 12 can be used for this purpose.

1   What have you had to give up and what have you gained in your relationship as a result of starting a family?

2   What were the high and low spots for each of you from pregnancy onwards?

3   What sort of things were most difficult to talk about with each other and with other people? Why do you think this was?

4   How did you decide upon who does what for the baby?

5   If either of you felt depressed or edgy before or after the baby was born, did you find it easier to talk it over with:

	Husband	Wife
— each other		
— friends		
— parents		
— doctor, midwife or health visitor		
— no-one		
— question does not apply		
Why do you think it was like this?		

6   In what ways was your sexual relationship affected by pregnancy and early parenthood?

7   Have you learned more about each other as a result of the baby? Have you learned more about your partnership? What sort of things—good and bad?

8   What effect has becoming a parent had on your own parents and on your relationship with them?

9   What sort of things has having a child brought back from your own remembered childhood feelings?

10 Was there help that you would have appreciated from some source that was not available to you?

or 10*

Were the discussion evenings of any help. If not, why not? What sort of help would you have liked?

11 From your experience, what would you most want to say to a couple starting a family?

12 Other comments:

* The variation of question ten was sent to those couples who were known to have attended one or more of the discussion evenings described in Chapter Four.

Therapeutic containment

A summary of the therapeutic process for the two marriages described in Chapter One

MR AND MRS GRANT

During the six-month period in which they met, Mr and Mrs Grant and their caseworkers paid attention to three aspects of their problem.

In the first place, the absence of a negotiating period in the marriage before Lisa was born suggested that the Grants should be seen together. This would establish a time and place for the two of them to meet, talk, and re-form their marriage. It was hoped that this would meet a need for what Mr Grant wistfully called 'late in the day pre-marital counselling'. As it turned out, they chose, with babysitting help from Mrs Grant's mother, to institute a regular weekly evening out together after their appointment at the Institute. This helped to reaffirm their marriage and strengthened its capacity to contain the tensions in their lives.

In the second place, and closely related to the first objective, attention was paid to the discrepancy between the Grants' tendency to hold themselves in reserve and the private hopes they entertained of each other in their marriage. This issue found a focus in discussion of their sexual relationship. Mrs Grant at first associated sex with having babies and, given the difficulties which had followed Lisa's birth, her sexual reluctance was understandable. However it became clear that Mrs Grant had enjoyed sex most when they were not using contraceptives and the risk of conception was at its highest. This apparent contradiction was interpreted in terms of the *idea* of a baby bringing Mrs Grant to life. Insofar as the tenderness and need for affection displayed by her husband represented the lost child within herself, the *idea* of a baby, rather like the *idea* of marriage, had associations for her with the chance of recovering aspects of her own childhood, not least the recovery of attention for herself. Why were these hopes not fulfilled?

In the course of therapy it became clear that there were risks for her in recovering that lost life. If she allowed herself to need others more, she ran the risk of loss and disappointment. The recovery of life risked the recovery of pain as well as joy. There were indications that, in tidying up her surroundings, Mrs Grant was attempting to keep her inner life under control. Abandoning herself to her feelings, and the loss of control implied, for example, by sexual orgasm, ran counter to the self-protective responses she had learned over the years.

The problem was not one-sided. Mr Grant observed that the self-sufficient qualities he saw in his wife made her a safe partner for himself. Her needs would not overtax his resources. Sexually, he had enjoyed her most after a period of separation, when he had recovered her from another man. Yet his passion, like hers, was kept secret, so that each was surprised to hear from the other when their feelings had been most intense. Mr Grant stood for wanting more warmth and affection, perhaps secure in the knowledge that his wife would remain cool. At first, while they were conscious only of the wish for warmth (expressed by Mr Grant) or for distance (expressed by Mrs Grant), the therapeutic process was geared towards raising awareness of these aspects of themselves to which each related in the other. Only then was there a chance of making safe in the marriage the expression of hopes which had previously been nurtured and protected in their private worlds.

Thirdly, through discussion an attempt was made to re-arrange family relationships in a way which would allow Mrs Grant more involvement with her daughter than had hitherto existed. In part, this connected with the work previously described and enabled Mr Grant to know that Lisa sometimes felt like 'a burden' as well as 'a shining light', and that when he feared being blamed by her at some time in the future, he was really talking about his wish to blame his own parents but his reluctance to do so.

Equally important, the re-arrangement of family relationships faced Mr and Mrs Grant with the task of evolving a parental identity with which they felt comfortable. Mr Grant had to come to terms with what he called 'this fathering business', accepting neither the distant model of his own father nor the indulgence which was born of an unsatisfied emotional craving of his own. For Mrs Grant, to involve herself more with Lisa implied some separation of her views from those of her mother, for example, by considering giving up work to become a full-time mother against her own mother's advice.

Outcome

Mrs Grant left the Institute resolved to give up work in order to look after Lisa. In preparing for a second child, she once again felt sexually responsive. Mr Grant left therapy with misgivings about whether or not they would be able to manage on their own.

He and his caseworker exchanged the occasional letter in the following year. During that time, the Grants moved into a larger flat and Mrs Grant gave up her job. She got in touch with her father and he came to stay with the family, a visit that Mr Grant enjoyed as much as his wife. It was clear from the letters that there were downs as well as ups, but that a significant shift had taken place in their partnership. Mr Grant expressed it in these terms:

> There is one change to record in my letter, so that you will know something of our life as a family; and that is my wife, now that she does not have a job to occupy her mind, certainly finds it much easier to be kind to Lisa. She might lose her temper now and again, much as many people do, but on the whole she is on very good terms with Lisa and talks to her and gives her things to do.
>
> Lisa still follows me about and makes the most she possibly can of me while I am at home; but I am afraid I am taking on some of the quickness of temper that my wife had before we moved, and find the child a nuisance more often, as she did. We have all noticed this, and it does show how things can change so greatly and in the most unexpected way.

MR AND MRS JACKSON

The help that Mr and Mrs Jackson received was directed towards grappling with some of the feelings and anxieties which the birth of a baby had stirred up in the marriage. They were in contact with the Institute for two and a half years. Their treatment divides naturally into two stages.

The first stage

After the preliminary interviews, Mr and Mrs Jackson were seen separately by two women caseworkers, neither of whom had conducted the earlier interviews.

Mr Jackson used his early sessions to lay emphasis upon a feeling that he had never really had 'fun' in his life, and to seek reassurance that his predicament and their marriage were 'normal'. He wished they might have a second child in order to demonstrate their normality.

After some weeks he expressed greater dissatisfaction with the marriage, claiming it had never really been right from the outset. He became increasingly anxious about how angry he felt towards his wife and his daughter. He thought his feelings were unreasonable, particularly as they were often precipitated by minor incidents, like his daughter turning away from him. He became frightened by the intensity of his reactions and wondered whether he needed to see a psychiatrist. Because they both shared some anxiety about the way he was feeling, a psychiatric consultation was arranged. The consultation helped to defuse the situation, although thereafter Mr Jackson began to cancel appointments, almost entirely withdrawing from treatment three months after he began.

The meaning of his withdrawal can be understood in two ways. In the first place, he had become very aware both of his need for attachment and his destructive impulses during the time he was seeing his caseworker. He was anxious about losing control of himself and may have withdrawn as a means of making life safer for all concerned. His fear of commitment in relationships can be understood in these terms. The conflict between the wish for an exclusive, positive attachment to another, and the fear of this attachment because it aroused mixed feelings from the past, was managed by preserving the wish in the world of fantasy and thereby guaranteeing against a further experience of loss.

The second explanation relates to changes taking place in the marriage. In this context, the bid for a psychiatric consultation, a bid once again to become the 'patient' in the marriage, might be seen as a move to restore the *status quo ante*. This latter possibility gains credence when account is taken of what was happening with Mrs Jackson. She and her caseworker were locked in something of a power struggle during the early stage of their relationship. 'Neither of us will give in,' remarked Mrs Jackson on one occasion, echoing a theme in her marriage and perhaps testing the robustness of her caseworker before taking things further.

As the weeks passed, she shifted her position in relation to her husband. At first she had talked of Mr Jackson as a troublesome thorn in her flesh which she would like to remove by leaving him. Later, she began to consider how anxious she would be if he decided to leave her. Abandoning the stance of one who copes, she began to become more depressed about herself. While this change was welcomed by her caseworker, it was clearly making things less comfortable at home. When she dissolved into tears, Mrs Jackson was aware of her husband hovering by the door, asking if she needed a doctor, and becoming concerned in case she 'did something silly'. However, in the face of her depression, she thought he was becoming more cheerful and optimistic than before. She was therefore surprised when he told her he was to have a psychiatric consultation for what he called 'depression', because she thought he was so much better. It frightened her at the time; she did not think she could live with his depression on top of her own.

Unlike her husband, Mrs Jackson stayed with her caseworker. She felt she received from her the mothering which helped her to mother Rose. Over the weeks it became clear how difficult it was for each partner to make time for the other in the marriage. Mr Jackson wanted to talk when he arrived home from a demanding day at work, but this coincided with Rose's bedtime and Mrs Jackson was not available to listen. When the bedtime routine was over and Mrs Jackson wanted to talk about her day, her husband was either behind the paper or engrossed in television. Likewise with sex: neither felt free to respond at the time when approached. The problem was graphically portrayed in a later interview when they talked together about the different significance food had for each of them: Mrs Jackson was particularly fond of her food, but felt

criticised by her husband every time she had a meal; Mr Jackson felt put off by
her appetite and said he could almost see her belly swelling after a meal. In his
eyes, her appetite was a demonstration of her lack of affection for him; if she
cared, she would slim. The extreme outcome seemed to be that for Mr Jackson
to be emotionally fed, his wife had to starve; alternatively, Mrs Jackson could
only be 'fed' at the expense of her husband.

As Mrs Jackson became more attached to her caseworker there were signs of
improvement both in herself and in the marriage. Nine months after they had
begun, the caseworker left the Institute of Marital Studies. The prospect of her
departure seemed to put the clock back. Once more there were angry exchanges
in the marriage (Mr Jackson returned to see his caseworker once because of this)
and Mrs Jackson again talked about divorce. Her caseworker worked hard to
make the connection between her departure and the anger Mrs Jackson felt
towards her which was being displaced into the marriage; after all, it was rather
as if her caseworker were 'divorcing' her. The connection was recognised by Mrs
Jackson, who on one occasion went further and directly related her desire to
start another baby with a wish to compensate for her caseworker's departure.
The intensity of her reaction, and its repercussions on the marriage, can be
understood in the context of the power of a caring relationship in the present to
re-evoke important relationships from the past. In this sense, it was as if Mrs
Jackson were losing her mother to someone else all over again.

It is likely that the improvement in the marriage had depended upon the
availability of Mrs Jackson's caseworker. Mr Jackson was then relieved of the
sole responsibility of supporting his wife, and her willingness to be looked after
by another woman may have increased her tolerance of him in two important
respects. In the first place, his needs then no longer competed so directly with
her own; in the second place, she no longer had, to the same degree, to
attribute to him needs which were her own. This may have had a freeing effect
on Mr Jackson and, indeed, upon Rose. The caseworker's departure threw all
this into reverse, and in view of the anxiety about managing alone, a renewed
offer of treatment was made to the Jacksons with different workers.

Before passing on to the second stage of treatment, it is relevant to consider
how Rose was affected by the changes which were taking place. Because Mrs
Jackson worked part-time, she employed a childminder. Early in the year, the
childminder left the family. Rose had been very attached to her and following
her departure she had showed signs of disturbance—withholding faeces and
refusing to go to sleep at night without someone in her room. Both these
symptoms suggested an inability to 'let go' which echoed the problems shared
by her parents. Suppositories were prescribed and one or both parents stayed
with her at night, which made things manageable if inconvenient. Mrs Jackson
connected the symptoms with the childminder's departure and thought they
would pass with time. However, when she was faced with the departure of her

own caseworker, her anxiety about Rose increased, and at her request their doctor referred Rose to a child guidance clinic. The clinic and the Institute were in touch with each other before the appointment was made. Subsequently, the clinic saw Mr and Mrs Jackson twice, focussing less upon their anxiety about Rose (who was not, in fact, seen) than upon their anxiety about themselves and each other. They, and particularly the reluctant Mr Jackson, were encouraged to return to the IMS for a further period. Rose's condition gradually improved.

The Second Stage

Mrs Jackson and her new worker had some interviews together before her husband returned to the IMS. These focussed in part upon Mrs Jackson's investment in keeping her husband out of treatment for fear that she might lose the attention she had secured by coming on her own. Mr Jackson wanted to talk to a man, and he eventually returned to see the caseworker who had first seen him. From then on the Jacksons were seen together, despite Mr Jackson's anxiety that speaking freely in his wife's presence might endanger the marriage.

The caseworkers decided to focus their attention upon the functions served by the different 'swellings' in the marriage. As far as they were understood, there were four identifiable and interrelated functions.

In the first place, they drew attention to the needs of each partner for care, support and reassurance. When Mr Jackson developed a mouth ulcer and asked his wife to look at it, he was drawing her attention to his real anxiety and asking her to take him seriously. Because this anxiety was expressed in terms of suspected cancer, for which there was no foundation, the request was self defeating, and increasingly so the more it was made. Similarly Mrs Jackson's swollen belly was associated for her with tension about keeping things in and managing alone. While Mr Jackson noticed her 'swelling' he misconstrued the meaning and failed to take sufficient account of her needs. Moreover, there was some collusion between them about where the swellings were most acceptable. Mrs Jackson reacted strongly when her belly was attacked, disguising her hurt and returning the attack. However, while he was concerned with *his* swellings, he would not attack hers. The swellings can therefore be said to represent an unmanageable burden of need, which in sense they 'agreed' should be vested in Mr Jackson.

Although the swellings made an appeal for care in the marriage, they ended up becoming the object of attack. While care was sought after, it was also feared in case it unleashed an overpowering neediness within the adults. A second function performed by the swellings can be seen as the control of the very needs they represented by creating psychological distance in the marriage. By preserving a belief that the needs were overwhelming (and cancer is a particularly evocative symbol for an agent which threatens to over-run the body and extinguish life itself), it became difficult to relate to any part of a request for help for fear the demand became absolute. In so far as there was a polarization between Mrs Jackson's need to be the caretaker and Mr Jackson's need to be cared for, the fear of becoming either the isolated parent or the needy child was experienced in a particularly acute way. Mrs Jackson felt robbed of emotional sustenance from her husband; Mr Jackson felt obsessed with himself and shut out from actively sharing in the parenting of his daughter.

Thirdly, the swellings protected Rose from her parents' negative feelings, feelings reactivated by past associations. In one sense she was the cause of the increased demands with which the family were having to contend, and was perhaps protected from her parents' anger at the cost of a higher level of dissatisfaction in the marriage. Mr Jackson's preoccupation with his wife's swollen belly can be seen as a displacement of his (in adult terms) unreasonably angry feelings towards Rose, the foetal 'lump' which had swollen Mrs Jackson during pregnancy. The feelings become more understandable when account is taken of the historical perspective: Mr Jackson's interpretation as a child of his mother's pregnancy, and the foetal swelling which was temporarily to banish him and permanently displace him from home. For Mrs Jackson, her reaction to the insistent demands represented by her husband's swellings was intensified by recollections of past situations when the needs of others had taken precedence over her own. The swellings can therefore be said to have 'stung' into consciousness the intense feelings associated with past loss and displacement, yet by becoming the object of attack they served to protect the real child, Rose, from their intensity.

In relation to this point, the caseworkers drew Mr and Mrs Jackson's attention to their difficulty in 'shutting the bedroom door', so to speak, and not allowing Rose to take over their lives. They suggested that the Jacksons' vulnerability to their daughter's crying demands stemmed from their identification with her predicament. This made it difficult for them to establish some space for themselves without fearing that they were attacking her and shutting her out in the cold in the same way as they themselves had felt shut out in the past. Slowly, some progress was made in establishing more appropriate boundaries, so that one or other parent did not have to spend the evening upstairs, and Mr Jackson less frequently changed places with his daughter so that she could share the marital bed with her mother.

Finally, it sometimes seemed as if the swellings were preserved as a kind of talisman against disaster by insuring that things remained bad; the pain of standing to lose the good experience which might follow improvement was thereby avoided. Mr Jackson was explicit about his 'black cloud' which dogged him everywhere and interfered with his enjoyment; if things started going well he was sure they would not last, and his conviction often turned out to be a self-fulfilling prophecy. As things improved in the marriage, both Mr and Mrs Jackson, but especially Mr Jackson, became increasingly anxious about whether the improvement could be sustained.

Outcome

Paradoxically, the tendency to ward off disaster by constantly being prepared for the worst was capable of precipitating what it was designed to avert. The attachment to dissatisfaction in the marriage occasionally triggered crises which stirred up intense feelings and brought the Jacksons' relationship to life in a precipitous way, raising the likelihood of real loss.

Following an improvement in the marriage and during the last summer of their treatment, a major crisis erupted. Mr Jackson decided he would leave his wife for a trial period of separation. The timing of his decision coincided with a break in treatment because of summer leave. It also coincided with the time Mrs Jackson had made an appointment with a gynaecologist to help her conceive a second child. Whether it was a decision to face the worst, or a reaction to the possibility of a further commitment, is not clear. Mr Jackson was, himself, puzzled, but thought that his 'black cloud' theory was relevant. During the period of separation he took the opportunity to test out his idea that there were green pastures elsewhere. His experience was not altogether reassuring. Mrs Jackson was upset and angry about her husband's departure and went abroad for a week. Mr Jackson repeatedly telephoned her while she was away.

When they returned to the IMS they were once again living together. Mrs Jackson was very angry about what had happened, not least with her caseworkers for being absent when they were most needed. Mr Jackson showed more commitment to the marriage than previously and wanted to invest in the future by having a second child. However, Mrs Jackson was back on the pill and planning to pick up the threads of her separate life. To the disappointment of her husband, she applied to continue the training she had interrupted for marriage, and her application was successful. This time, the Jacksons did not make it an issue of absolute choice (marriage or career) and Mr Jackson was able to tolerate his sense of being excluded by her training prospects. Having secured both a place on a course and her husband's acceptance of her intentions, Mrs Jackson decided not to take up the place she had been offered. Instead, she came off the pill.

Mr Jackson became less anxious about his cancer phobia. At first his wife resented this; she thought he was being 'secretive' and viewed his occasional medical consultations rather as if he were conducting an affaire behind her back. On one occasion, her fears had more substance: she felt particularly jealous when he agreed to have lunch with an old girl-friend whom he had not seen for years. Instead of holding in the very strong feelings this event aroused in her, she allowed them to find their way back into the marriage with the result that they discovered a passion in their sexual relationship which had previously been absent.

Even their caseworkers were invited to experience what it felt like to be left out in the cold! Mr Jackson decided he would consult a behavioural psychiatrist to see if a conditioning approach to his symptoms would remove his fear of cancer. The issue was raised by him as if he might have to choose between alternative therapies. The caseworkers agreed that such a choice was not necessary and he consulted the psychiatrist as he had proposed. The offer of treatment was not followed up. At the point at which contact with the Institute ended, Mr Jackson was much less concerned about his health, although not completely free of his fear of lumps. He felt he could 'look forward with confidence to another five or ten years of life, instead of another week or month'.

Table I Response to the programmes of group meetings

Name of Health Centre	Programme no.	No. of invitations issued to couples*	Predominant method of invitation	Response by couples to meetings†							Total no. of participant couples
				Ante-natal				Post-natal			
				1	2	3	4	1	2	3	
Mattock Lane	1	20	Letter/form	6	5	2		3	2	1	7
	2	12	Letter/form	1	0		Programme discontinued				1
	3	13	Letter/form	3	2		Programme discontinued				3
	4	7	Letter/form	1	0		Programme discontinued				1
Laurel House	1	5	Indiv. cont.	4	4	2 (1)		2	2	1	4
	2	6	Indiv. cont.	6	5	3		5	3	2	6
Hanwell	1	10	Letter & group contact	2	0	1	1	Programme discontinued			3
	2	26	Letter	5 (3)	4 (3)	3 (3)	3 (2)	4 (1)	2 (1)	2	7 (3)
	3	19	Letter	2	1	1	Programme discontinued				2
Islip Manor	1	9	Letter & group contact	2 (1)	1 (1)	0	Programme discontinued				3 (2)
	2	8	group contact	3 (1)	3	2		2	2	1	4
	3	4	group contact	2	2	Programme not proceeded with					2
	4	4	group contact	Programme not proceeded with							0
	5	7	group contact	Programme not proceeded with							0
	6	30	Indiv. cont.	7 (4)	7	3 (2)	3	3	1	1	9 (2)

* These figures represent the minimum number of invitations known to have been issued. As some invitations were issued and not recorded the actual figures will be marginally higher. † Figures in brackets indicate women who attended alone, and are additional to those indicating couple response

Table II   Age and social class characteristics of those who attended programmes which ran full-term *

Name of Health Centre	Programme no.	Known age span of mothers	Estimate of average age	I	II	Social Class III	IV	V	NK
Mattock Lane	1	26—35	30.5†	1	4				2
Laurel House	1	All over 30	over 30		4				
	2	25—38†	31.5†	2	3	1			
Hanwell	2	25—37	30.3		6	3			1
Islip Manor	2	28—35†	31.5†		2	1			1
	6	20—32	27†	1	3	3			4

* *Source*: Office of Population Consensus & Surveys (1970); Classification of Occupations. HMSO. Figures based on wife's occupation or, when not known, that of her husband.
† Indicates that information was incomplete; the figures are based on what was known.

Institute of Marital Studies/Health Visitors' Workshops

Task: To study the effect on the marriage relationship of a first baby and its implications for the role of the health visitor.

The birth of a baby has significance in the context of his parents' past and present relationships which may critically affect their ability to behave as they might wish or plan in relation to their infant. The way the transition to parenthood is managed is profoundly affected by the nature of the couple's marriage, as is the marriage affected by the transition itself.

1   It is hoped that each workshop will be valued as a joint enterprise, with the IMS workers and the health visitors having a shared investment in the task.

2   The focus of each workshop will be on studying and attempting to understand the ways different couples interact together over the arrival of a first baby, the problems that are confronted, how they are managed and the response each couple makes to the health visitor. It is anticipated that health visitors will present details of their normal observations and work with couples expecting, or who have recently produced, their first baby, whether or not these couples present as 'problems'.

3   Special consideration will be given to understanding the problems of picking up and responding to stress signals emitted by a couple having their first baby and the problems inherent in offering appropriate help to couples who find difficulty making the transition to parenthood without neglecting their relationship with each other. Close attention will be paid to the potential of the health visitor for containing these tensions without referral, although the 'when' and 'how' of making a referral will also be considered.

4   Each workshop will be led by two of the IMS workers and will meet weekly for 1½ hours for 5 periods of 8—10 weeks throughout the project. Membership will be open only to those who expect to be able to attend regularly for all five periods.

5   The case material presented will be regarded as confidential to the workshop. The use of any case material in future publications will be presented in a disguised form and worked through by the IMS workers with the health visitor responsible for the case. The work content of the workshop as a whole may not be used for any other publication without the consent of the IMS.

Characteristics of Workshop cases * *and Health Visitors' Contacts*

Table I   Age of youngest baby and explicit reference to marital stress when case first presented for discussion

	6 wks and under	7 wks to 3 m	Over 3 m to 5 m	6- m	9 m to 1 yr	over 1 yr	Not known	Total
Explicit reference	2 (0)*	2 (1)	6 (5)	5 (4)	2 (2)	6 (4)	0	23 (16)
No explicit reference	17 (12)	6 (6)	1 (1)	6 (6)	7 (6)	2 (1)	2 (2)	41 (34)
Total	19 (12)	8 (7)	7 (6)	11 (10)	9 (8)	8 (5)	2 (2)	64 (50)

Table II   Social class of cases by wife's occupation†

Workshop venue	I	II	III	IV	V	Armed Services	Not known	Total
Mattock Lane	4	15	9	3	0	0	6	37
Hanwell	1	6	13	2	0	1	4	27
Total	5	21	22	5	0	1	10	64

Table III   Social class and explicit reference to marital stress by one or more family members

		I	II	III	IV	V	Armed Services	Not known	Total
Figures	Explicit reference	1	6	9	1	0	1	5	23
	No explicit reference	4	15	13	4	0	0	5	41
	Total	5	21	22	5	0	1	10	64
As % of relevant group	% of 'explicit' group	4.4	26.0	39.1	4.4	0	4.4	21.7	100
	% of 'no reference' group	9.8	36.5	31.7	9.8	0	0	12.2	100
	% of total group	7.8	32.8	34.4	7.8	0	1.6	15.6	100

* Figures in brackets indicate mothers who had not previously had a live birth.
† Based on the Office of Censuses & Population Classification of Occupations, 1970. If a woman's occupation was not known (i.e. her occupation prior to becoming a mother), that of her husband was used as the basis for classification.

Table IV Age of wife when case was first presented for discussion

Workshop venue	30 +	28-29	25-27	22-24	21 and under	Not known	Total
Mattock Lane	11 (8)*	11 (8)	3 (1)	4 (3)	3 (3)	5 (5)	37 (28)
Hanwell	11 (8)	5 (4)	5 (5)	3 (2)	3 (3)	0	27 (22)
Total	22 (16)	16 (12)	8 (6)	7 (5)	6 (6)	5 (5)	64 (50)

Table V Reference to ante-natal contact with mothers and to any contact with fathers

Workshop venue	Contact as confirmed by workshop notes	Ante-natal contact	Contact with Father
Mattock Lane	Contact	15 (13)*	25 (20)
	No contact	14 (9)	4 (2)
	No reference either way	8 (6)	8 (6)
Hanwell	Contact	10 (8)	12 (10)
	No contact	4 (4)	3 (3)
	No reference either way	13 (10)	12 (9)

* Figures in brackets indicate those mothers who had not previously had a live birth.

Note: The factual pen-pictures drawn by these tables will contain a margin of error. Health visitors relied upon memory as well as records to supply details of their cases. In one or two instances details were not known but were categorised because the health visitor concerned had a clear impression of the group to which she thought a particular family belonged.

References

Bain, A (1978)   The Capacity of Families to Cope with Transitions: A Theoretical Essay. *Human Relations* **31**, 675–88.

Bain, A (1976)   Presenting Problems in Social Consultancy: Three Case Histories concerning the selection of managers. *Human Relations* **29**, 643–57.

Balint, M (1964)   The Doctor, his Patient and the Illness (2nd ed.). London. Pitman Medical.

Balint, E (1972)   Fair Shares and Mutual Concern. *Int. Jnl. Psych.Anal.* **53**, 61–5.

Ballou, J W (1978)   *The Psychology of Pregnancy.* Lexington, Mass.

Bax, M (1976)   Are Mothers Necessary? *The Listener,* 7 Oct.–25 Nov.

Bibring, G L (1959)   Some Consideration of the Psychological Processes in Pregnancy. *Psychoanal. Study of Child.* **14**, 113–21.

Blood, R O and Wolfe, D M (1960)   *Husbands and Wives. The Dynamics of Married Living.* Glencoe Ill.: Free Press.

Bott, E (1971)   Family and Crisis. In Sutherland, J D (ed) *Towards Community Mental Health.* Tavistock.

Bradburn, N M and Caplovitz, D (1965)   *Reports on Happiness: a Pilot Study of Behaviour Related to Mental Health.* Chicago: Aldine.

Brearley, P *et al* (1978)   *The Social Context of Health Care.* Blackwell and Mott.

Breen, D (1975)   *The Birth of a First Child.* Tavistock.

Brimblecombe, F S W *et al* (1975)   in *Bridging in Health: Reports of Studies in Health Services for Children.* Ed McLachlan, G. London: OUP for the Nuffield Provincial Hospitals Trust.

Brown, G W *et al* (1975) Social Class and Psychiatric Disturbance among Women in an Urban Population. *Sociology* **9**, 225–54.

Brown, G W and Harris, T (1978)   *Social Origins of Depression.* Tavistock.

Brown, W A and Shereshefsky, P (1972)   Seven Women: A Prospective Study of Post-Partum Psychiatric Disorder. *Psychiatry* **35**, 139–59.

Burr, W R (1970)   Satisfaction with Various Aspects of Marriage over the Life Cycle. *Jnl. Marriage and Family,* **32**, 29–37.

Byng-Hall, J (1973)   Family Myths used as a Defence in Conjoint Family Therapy. *Br. Jnl. Med. Psychol,* **46**, 239–50.

Caplan, G (1951)   Mental Hygiene Work with Expectant Mothers: A Group-Therapeutic Approach. *Mental Hygiene* **35**, 41–50.

Caplan, G (1961)   *An Approach to Community Mental Health.* London: Tavistock.

Caplan, G (1964)   *Principles of Preventive Psychiatry.* London: Tavistock.

Caplan, G (1978)   Family Support Systems in a Changing World. In Anthony E J and Chiland, C (eds), *Children and their Parents in a Changing World* New York: Chichester, Wiley.

Carroll, Lewis *Alice's Adventures in Wonderland.*

Cartwright, A (1975) *The Dignity of Labour.* Futura Books.
Central Statistical Office (1982) *Social Trends.* HMSO.
Chertok, L *et al* (1969) *Motherhood and Personality.* London: Tavistock.
Cochrane, N. (1973) Some Reflections on the Unsuccessful Treatment of a Group of Married Couples. *Brit. Jnl. of Psychiatry* 123, 395–401.
Cohen, M G (1966) Personal Identity and Sexual Identity. *Psychiatry* 29, 1–12.
Court, S D M—Chmn. (1976) *Fit for the Future.* The Report of the Committee on Child Health Services. London: HMSO.
Curtis, J L (1955) A Psychological Study of 55 Expectant Fathers. *US Armed Forces Med. Jnl.* 6, 937–950.
Cyr, F E and Wattenberg, S H (1965) Social Work in a Preventive Program of Medical and Child Health. In Parad, H J (ed), *Crisis Intervention: Selected Readings.* Family Service Assoc. of Am.
Dalton, K (1971) Prospective Study into Puerperal Depression. *Br. Jnl. Psych.* 118, 689–92.
Daniels, R S and Smith, R (1979) Changing Functions of the Family: Their Inter-relationships with Health and Illness. In Wood, C (ed), *Health and the Family.* Academic Press.
Dept. of Ed. and Science (1977) *Education in Schools.* Green Paper, London: HMSO.
Dept. of Health and Social Security (1974) *Preparation for Parenthood.*London: HMSO; (1974) *Dimensions of Parenthood.* London: HMSO; (1978) *Violence to Children.* White Paper. London: HMSO.
Deutsch, H (1944, 1945) *Psychology of Women. A Psycho-Analytic Interpretation.* Vols I and II. New York: Grune and Stratton.
Dicks, H V (1967) *Marital Tensions.* Routledge and Kegan Paul.
Douglas, G (1968) Some Emotional Disorders of the Puerperium. *Jnl. Psychosomatic Research* 12, 101–6.
Dumon, W A (1978) Two Become Three. Paper presented at the Commission on Marriage and Marriage Guidance (IUFO) Conference entitled *Two Become Three.* Vienna, 9–12 June.
Dyer, E D (1963) Parenthood as Crisis: A Re-study. *Marriage and Family Living* 25, 196–201.
Edgell, S (1980) *Middle-class couples.* Allen and Unwin.
Eliot, T S *The Journey of the Magi.* London: Faber and Faber.
Erikson, E H (1959) *Identity and the Life Cycle.* New York: Int. Univs. Press.
Evans, S L *et al* (1972) Failure to Thrive: A Study of 45 children and their Families. *Jnl. Child Psych.* 11, 440–57.
Falicov, C J (1971) *Interpersonal Reorganizations during Pregnancy and Motherhood.* University of Chicago (unpublished thesis).
Farnese, M (1978) We All Work for a Dinosaur. *Nursing Mirror* (30 Nov. 1978), p. 55.
Feldman, H (1971) The Effects of Children on the Family. In Michael, A (ed), *Family Issues of Employed Women in Europe and America.* Leider, Brill.
Finer, M (Chmn) (1974) *The Report of the Committee on One-Parent Families.* Cmnd 5629 HMSO.
Freud, S 1896 Further Remarks on the Neuro-Psychoses of Defence (Phrase first used in this paper; see standard edition (Hogarth Press, 1962), vol III, p. 170.)

Frommer, E A and O'Shea, G (1973a)   Ante-natal Identification of Women liable to have Problems in Managing their Infants. *British Journal of Psychiatry*, 123, 149–56.

Frommer, E A and O'Shea, G (1973b)   The Importance of Childhood Experience in relation to Problems of Marriage and Family Building. *Br. Jnl. Psych.* 123, 157–60.

Gaddini, E (1976)   On 'Father Formation' in Early Child Development. *Int. Jnl. Psycho-anal.* 57, 397.

Gavron, H (1968)   *The Captive Wife.* Pelican Books.

Gelder, M G (1978)   Endocrine Status and Post-Natal Depression. Paper given at the Institute of Obstetrics and Gynaecology's Symposium on *Mental Illness in Pregnancy and the Puerperium.* 2 March.

Gelles, R J (1975)   Violence and Pregnancy: A Note on the Extent of the Problem and Needed Services. *Family Co-ordinator* 24, 81–6.

Gennep, van, A (1960)   The Rites of Passage. Routledge and Kegan Paul.

Gordon, R E and Gordon, K K (1959)   Social Factors in the Prediction and Treatment of Emotional Disorders of Pregnancy. *Am. Jnl. of Obstetrics and Gynaecology,* 77, 1074–83.

Gordon, R E and Gordon, K K (1960)   Social Factors in the Prevention of Post-partum Emotional Problems. *Obstet. and Gynaecol.* 15, 433–8.

Gordon, R E *et al* (1965)   Factors in Post-partum Emotional Adjustment, *Obstet. and Gynaecol.* 25, 158–66.

Goshen-Gottstein, E R (1966)   *Marriage and the First Pregnancy.* London: Tavistock.

Green, A H *et al* (1974)   Child Abuse: Pathological Syndrome of Family Interaction. *Am. Jnl. Psych.* 131, 882–6.

Hamilton, J A (1962)   *Postpartum Psychiatric Problems.* St Louis: Mosby.

Health Visitors Association, 1975. *Health Visiting in the Seventies.*

Hicks, D (1976)   *Primary Health Care.* HMSO.

Hinchcliffe, M K, Hooper, D and Roberts, F J (1978)   *The Melancholy Marriage.* John Wiley and Sons.

Hiskins, G (1980)   *How Mothers Help Themselves.* A Study of Post-Natal Support Groups. Unpublished document.

Hobbs, D F (1965)   Parenthood as Crisis: A Third Study. *Jnl. Marriage and The Family* 27, 367–72.

Hobbs, D F (1968)   Transition to Parenthood: A Replication and an Extension. *Jnl. Marriage and the Family* 30, 413–17.

Hobbs, D F and Cole, S P (1976)   Transition to Parenthood: A Decade Replication. *Jnl. Marriage and the Family* 38, 723–31.

Hobbs, D F and Wimbish, J M (1977)   Transition to Parenthood by Black Couples. *Jnl. Marriage and the Family* 39, 677–89.

Home Office, Dept. Health and Social Security (1979)   *Marriage Matters.* HMSO.

Illich, I (1975)   *Medical Nemesis,* Calder and Boyars.

Jacoby, A D (1969)   Transition to Parenthood: A Reassessment. *Jnl. Marriage and the Family* 31, 720–7.

Janis, I L (1958)   *Psychological Stress.* New York: Wiley.

Janis, I L (1968)   When Fear is Healthy. *Psychol. Today,* 1, 46–9, 60–1.

Karpf, A (1979)   Leaving Father in at the Birth. *Observer* (14 Jan. 1979).

Kennedy, I (1980)   *Unmasking Medicine,* Reith Lectures. BBC publication.

Klosterman, G (1976)   In Bax (ed), Are Mothers Necessary? *The Listener* (18 Nov. 1976).
Lacousiere, R B (1972)   Fatherhood and Mental Illness. A Review and New Material. *Psychiatric Quarterly* **46**, 109–24.
Landis, J T *et al* (1952)   Effects of First Pregnancy on Sex Adjustment. In Landis, J T and Landis, M G (eds), *Readings in Marriage and the Family*, pp. 228–34. New York: Prentice-Hall.
La Rossa, R (1977)   *Conflict and Power in Marriage. Expecting the First Child.* Beverly Hills/London. Sage Publications.
Laslett, B (1973)   The Family as a Public and Private Institution: An Historical Perspective. *Jnl. Marriage and the Family* **35**, 480–90.
Le Masters, E E (1957)   Parenthood as Crisis. *Marriage and Family Living* **19**, 352–5.
Leonard, D (1980)   *Sex and Generation: a Study of Courtships and Weddings.* Tavistock.
Lerner, R M and Spanier, G B (ed) (1978)   *Child Influences on Marital and Family Interaction.* Academic Press.
Levinson, D J (1978)   *The Seasons of a Man's Life.* New York: A A Knopf.
Lewis, E (1976)   The Atmosphere in the Labour Ward. *Jnl. Child Psychotherapy* **4 (2)** 89–92.
Lindemann, E (1944)   Symptomatology and Management of Acute Grief. *Am. Jnl. Psychiatry,* **101**, 141–8.
Luckey, E B and Bain, J K (1970)   Children: A Factor in Marital Satisfaction. *Jnl. Marriage and the Family* **32**, 43–4.
Macfarlane, A (1977)   *The Psychology of Childbirth.* Fontana.
Marris, P (1974)   *Loss and Change.* Routledge and Kegan Paul.
Masters, W H and Johnson, V E (1966)   *Human Sexual Response.* London: Churchill.
Mattinson, J (1975)   *The Reflection Process in Casework Supervision.* IMS
Mattinson, J and Sinclair, I (1979)   *Mate and Stalemate.* Blackwells.
Mead, M (1962)   *Male and Female.* Pelican Books.
Menzies, I E P (1970)   *The Functioning of Social Systems as a Defence Against Anxiety.* Tavistock Institute of Human Relations.
Merrison, A (Chmn) (1979)   Royal Commission on the National Health Service, HMSO.
Meyerowitz, J H and Feldman, H (1966)   Development of the Husband–Wife Relationship. A Research Report. Referred to in Dumon, W A (op. cit.).
Minuchin, S (1974)   *Families and Family Therapy.* London, Tavistock.
Morris, B (1971)   An Educational Perspective on Mental Health. In Sutherland, J D (ed), *Towards Community Mental Health.* Tavistock.
Oakley, A (1974)   *The Sociology of Housework.* Martin Robertson.
Oakley, A (1979a)   The Baby Blues. *New Society,* 5 April.
Oakley, A (1979b)   *Becoming a Mother.* Martin Robertson.
Oakley, A (1980)   *Women Confined.* Martin Robertson.
Office of Population Consensus and Surveys (1970)   *Classification of Occupations.* HMSO.
Ortho-Pharmaceutical Films Ltd *Sexuality and Communication.*
Parad, H J and Caplan, G (1965)   A Framework for Studying Families in Crisis. In Parad, H J (ed), *Crisis Intervention: Selected Readings.* Family Service Assoc. of America.

Parkes, C M (1971) Psycho-Social Transitions: A Field for Study. *Social Science and Medicine*, **5**, 101–15.
Parkes, C M (1979) The Use of Community Care in Prevention. In Meacher, M (ed) *New Methods of Mental Health Care*. Pergamon Press.
Pincus, L (ed) (1960) *Marriage: Studies in Emotional Conflict and Growth*. Institute of Marital Studies, London.
Pines, D (1978) On Becoming a Parent. *Jnl. Child Psychotherapy*, **4**, 19–31.
Pitt, B (1968) A typical Depression following Childbirth. *Br. Jnl. Psychiatry* **114**, 1325–35.
Pitt, B (1973) Maternal Blues. *Br. Jnl. Psychiatry* **122**, 431–3.
Powell, A (1971) *Books Do Furnish a Room*. Heinemann.
Pringle, K M (1980) In Pugh, G (ed), *Preparation for Parenthood*. National Children's Bureau.
Pugh, G (1980) *Preparation for Parenthood: Some Current Initiatives*. National Children's Bureau.
Rainwater, L (1960) *And the Poor Get Children*. New York: Watts.
Rapoport, R (1965) Normal Crisis, Family Structure and Mental Health. In Parad, H J (ed), *Crisis Intervention: Selected Readings*. Family Service Assoc. of America.
Rapoport, L (1965a) The State of Crisis: Some Theoretical Considerations. In Parad, H J (ed), *Crisis Intervention: Selected Readings*. Family Service Assoc. of America.
Rapoport, L (1965b) Working with Families in Crisis: An Exploration in Preventive Intervention. In Parad, H J (ed), *Crisis Intervention: Selected Readings*. Family Service Assoc. of America.
Rapoport, R and Rapoport, R (1968) Family Transitions in Contemporary Society. *Jnl. Psychosomatic Research* **12**, 29–38.
Rapoport, R and Rapoport, R (1971) *Dual Career Families*. Penguin.
Rapoport, R *et al* (1977) *Fathers, Mothers and Others*. Routledge and Kegan Paul.
Richards, M (1980) Husbands Become Fathers. Paper given at a conference on the *Impact of Children on Marriage*. UK. Marriage Research Centre, 23 April.
Richman, J, Goldthorp, W O and Simmons, C (1975) Fathers in Labour. *New Society*, 16 October.
Richman, N (1974) Effects of Housing on Pre-school Children and their Mothers. *Devel/opt. Med. and Child Neurol.* **16**, 53–7.
Richman, N (1976) Depression in Mothers of Pre-School Children. *Jnl. Child Psychol. and Psychiat.* **17**, 75–8.
Richter, H E (1976) Role of Family Life in Child Development. *Int. Jnl. Psychoanal.* **57**, 385.
Robin, A A (1962) The Psychological Changes of Normal Parturition. *Psych. Quarterly* **36**, 129–50.
Rollins, B C and Feldman, H (1970) Marital Satisfaction over the Life Cycle. *Jnl. Marriage and the Family* **32**, 20–8.
Rollins, B C and Galligan, R (1978) The Developing Child and Marital Satisfaction of Parents. In Lerner, R M and Spanier, G B (ed) (op. cit.).
Rossi, A S (1968) Transition to Parenthood. *Jnl. Marriage and the Family*, **30**, 26–39.
Russell, C S (1974) Transition to Parenthood: Problems and Gratifications. *Jnl. Marriage and the Family* **36**, 294–301.

Rutter, M (1974)   Dimensions of Parenthood: Some Myths and Some Suggestions. In *The Family in Society: Dimension of Parenthood*. DHSS Seminar. HMSO.

Rutter, M and Madge, M (1976)   *Cycles of Disadvantage*. London: Heinemann.

Ryder, R G (1973)   Longitudinal Data relating Marriage Satisfaction and Having a Child. *Jnl. Marriage and the Family* 35, 604–6.

Scott, P D (1974)   Battered Wives. *Br. Jnl. Psychiatry* 125, 433–41.

Seligman, M E P (1975)   *Helplessness*. San Francisco: Freeman.

Sheehy, G (1977)   *Passages: Predictable Crises of Adult Life*. Bantam Books.

Shereshefsky, P M and Yarrow, L J (1973)   *Psychological Aspects of a First Pregnancy and early Post-natal Adaptation*. New York: Raven Press.

Sinclair, I (1975)   *Marriage and Birth of a Baby: Preliminary Literature Survey*. Institute of Marital Studies. (Unpublished paper.)

Skynner, A C R (1973)   Letter, *Br. Jnl. Psychiatry,* 123, 124.

Stone, L (1977)   *The Family, Sex and Marriage in England 1500–1800*. Weidenfeld and Nicolson.

Sutherland, J D (1962)   Introduction to *The Marital Relationship as a Focus for Casework*. Institute of Marital Studies. London.

Sutherland, J D Object Relations Theory and the Conceptual Model of Psychoanalysis. *Br. Jn. Med. Psychol.* (1963), 36, 109–24.

Sutherland, J D (1971)   *Towards Community Mental Health*. London: Tavistock.

Thompson, A G (1960)   In Pincus, L (ed), *Marriage: Studies in Emotional Conflict and Growth,* Institute of Marital Studies.

Thornes, B and Collard, J (1979)   *Who Divorces?* Routledge and Kegan Paul.

Thornton, A (1977)   Children and Marital Stability. *Jnl. of Marriage and the Family* 39, 531–40.

Trethowan, W H (1968)   The Couvade Syndrome—Some Further Observations. *Jnl. Psych. Research* 12, 107–15.

Tweedie, J (1979)   In *The Guardian*, 19 April 1979.

Udenberg, N (1974)   Psychological Aspects of Sexual Inadequacy in Women. *Jnl. Psychosomatic Research* 18, 33–47.

Watson, P (1977)   Why Babies bring the 'Blues'. *Sunday Times,* 20 February.

Wenner, N K et al (1969)   Emotional Problems in Pregnancy. *Psychiatry* 32, 389–410.

Whitehead, L (1976)   *Early Parenthood: Its Consequences for Firstborns in a National Survey*. Unpublished thesis.

Wilson, A T M (1961)   Comments on: A Sociological and Psychoanalytic Study of 20 London Marriages. Paper given at the *Fourth World Congress on Sociology*. Stresa.

Wilson, A R (1968)   An Investigation into the Psychological Aspects of Pregnancy and the Puerperium Using the Technique of Group Analysis. *Jnl. Psychosomatic Research* 12, 73–82.

Winnicott, D W (1956)   Primary Maternal Preoccupation. In *Through Paediatrics to Psycho-analysis*. (1958), pp. 300–5. Tavistock.

Winnicott, D W (1964)   *The Child, the Family and the Outside World*. Penguin.

Winnicott, D W (1971)   The Concept of a Healthy Individual. In Sutherland, J D (ed), *Towards Community Mental Health*. Tavistock.

Woodhouse, D L (1975)   Personal Development and Marital Interaction. *Marriage Guidance* 15, 359–68.

Whitfield, R C (1980)   *Education for Family Life*. Hodder and Stoughton.

Zacijek, E and Wolkind, S (1978)   Emotional Difficulties in Married Women During and After the First Pregnancy. *Br. Jnl. Med. Psychol.* 51, 379–85.

South East Essex College

of Arts & Technology
Luker Road, Southend-on-Sea, Essex, SS1 1ND.
Tel: (01702) 220400 Fax: (01702) 432320 Minicom: (01702) 220642